50/50

Poems & Translations by Womxn over 50

Edited by
Ann Davenport

Quills Edge Press

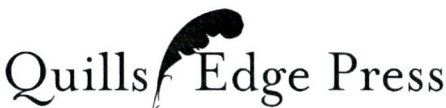

Published by QuillsEdge Press
quillsedgepress.org

Anthology selection © 2018 by QuillsEdge Press
"Why Poetry?" © 2018 by Ann Davenport
All rights information: editor@quillsedgepress.org

Cover and book design by Ann Davenport
Printed in the United States of America
First Edition

ISBN 978-0-9967424-6-7

Quail's Edge Press

Thank you for supporting ce...

Make a tax-deductible, year-end indispensable gift to help us publish more indispensable poetry by women over 50!

Donate securely at quailsedgepress.org

Carol Amato
Laura Apol
Pam Baggett
P. V. Beck
Nan Becker
Virginia Bell
Brenda Bell Brown
Wendy Taylor Carlisle
Nívea Castro
Sue Churchill
Wendy Mitman Clarke
Kimberly A. Collins
Tricia Coscia
Arfah Daud
Christine Ernst
Joanne Esser
Joanne Godley
Ruth Goring
Pamela Gibbs Hirschler
Susan Hodgin
Akua Lezli Hope
Kate Hovey
JP Howard
Siham Karami
Helena Kim

...niry
...Miller
Ruth Mota
Bo Niles
Faith Paulsen
Nadine Pinede
Phyllis Price
Julie Rochlin
Joanna Rose
Katherine DiBella Seluja
Margie Shaheed
Amy Small-McKinney
Rose M. Smith
Judith Sornberger
Lynne Santy Tanner
Eileen Toomey
Gina Valdés
Lynn Valente
Wendy Marie Vergoz
Tori Grant Welhouse

Why Poetry?

What would happen if one woman told the truth about her life?
The world would split open.—Muriel Rukeyser

What began as thinking we might have some interest if we offered an anthology of poetry by womxn over 50 quickly turned into an avalanche of nearly 600 submissions.

So many poems of survival, of witness, of longing, celebration, castigation. So much pain, courage, heartbreak, resilience, love. So many truths splitting the world open.

Along with their poems, each anthologist offers an answer to the question, "Why poetry?" The answers are infinite. For me, poetry is an inexorable need of the soul. In an age when people are pushed to consume rather than create, writing poetry is an act of resistance. Poetry, like any art, allows us to be vulnerable and powerful at the same time. It allows us to speak our truth with clarity, and to bring clarity to that which defies language. Great poems don't start as answers; they start as questions. The act of exploration that we call writing poetry is an act of courage, curiosity, and connection.

Speaking of connection: why spell women as womxn? The inclusive word "womxn" encompasses all self-identifying women of all cultures. It is more crucial than ever that historically silenced voices be amplified, including those of womxn of color, genderqueer womxn, refugees, immigrants, and others who have been cast as Other by our country's mores. We offer this intersectional anthology to honor and amplify. We are humbled to be entrusted with the hearts' truths of the poets featured here.

Creating this anthology has been a process built with deep gratitude. Thank you to each womxn who submitted their work. Thank you to the anthologists, who responded to every request and update with grace and encouragement. Thank you to all who supported the Press behind the scenes —to Anu Mahadev for her many contributions; to our many dedicated readers, who spent untold hours poring over the submissions; to our eternally supportive Board of Directors, Jude-Laure Denis, Molly Wingate, and Chelsea Palermo; to our founders, Elliott batTzedek and especially Jane Seitel, whose vision launched this anthology; and to other friends who gave advice and support whenever needed, especially Roberto Garcia, Myra McGovern, and Heather Huffman. And never least, endless thanks to my family for their enduring love and patience.

And thank you, who now hold this in your hands. May it split your world open.

Ann Davenport
Manitou Springs, Colorado

Table of Contents

Laura Apol
    The Fox   3
    Instructions for the Friends Who Are Sorting My Daughter's   4
        Things This Afternoon

Pam Baggett
    How Fathers Leave   5
    Remorse   6

Brenda Bell Brown
    keep a messy house   7
    We All Gots to Git   8
    Sister. Girl.   9

Christine Ernst
    fold   10
    cognate means blood-related   13
    cradle   14

Faith Paulsen
    Poem in Response to Steve Nolan   16
    Venus   17

Tori Grant Welhouse
    Lesson Eighteen   18
    Lesson Twenty-One   19
    Lesson Twenty-Two   20

Amy Small-McKinney
    Poem Beginning with a Line by Daisy Zamora   21
    In Our World   22
    Treatment for Panic, Low-Grade and Chronic   23

Mary Catherine Loving
    Regarding my actions over the past week   24
    A Slave Woman Recalls the Affair   26
    Interplanetary Love Jones   27

JC Miller
    X   29
    To My Husband and Other Strangers   30
    Honey the Air   31

Nan Becker
    Suddenly, and then suddenly...   32
    The color lent by the sky...   33

Gail Langstroth
    Number 2, Manhattan-bound Bronx train   34
    Negative Incursions: Rula Halawani's Photograph   36
    The Farmhand Lost His Voice   37

Rose M. Smith
    Blood from the Son   38
    Mourning Season   40
    take   41

Janet MacFadyen
    After   43
    Feeding the Peat Stove   44
    When I Understood   45

Ruth Goring
    Cancioncitas de remiendas/Small songs for mending   46
    The run-on sentences of Saramago   48
    Message   49

Helena Kim
    Field of Possibility   50
    Pele's Fire   51
    Paper Shirt, Paper Pants   52

Phyllis Price
    The Shepherd's Wife   53
    Mesa Dreams   54
    Blessing of the Old Horse   55

Nadine Pinede
    Note to Self   56
    Water Bearers: Summer 2016   57

    Stones in the Sun   59

Katharyn Howd Machan
    Bright Speck   62
    French Coffee   63

Siham Karami
    Elvira   65
    Interconnected   66
    Romancing the Muse   67

Carol Amato
    Good-Hearted Woman   68
    Nocturne II: Day's End   69
    Lily: Her Cancer   70

Wendy Taylor Carlisle
    Make it Up   71
    All of Them   72
    In the Year of Our Lord   73

Nívea Castro
    Brujas   74
    Tango   75
    Told   76

JP Howard
    complicated praise poem for sugar hill, harlem & her secrets   77
    Love is a woman   78
    Two Tankas for Trayvon's Mom   79

Katherine DiBella Seluja
    Wild Daisies   80
    As she had planned   81
    Harvest   82

Joanne Esser
    View at Fifty-Five   83
    Summer Accounting   84

Judith Sornberger
    On Letting Myself Go Gray   85

    This Autumn Morning Arrays Itself   86
    Just This Once, Just This Much   87

P.V. Beck
    Rivers   88
    The Seam of Time   89
    Out of Place   90

Susan Hodgin
    October Mourning   91
    Sub, Assigned Drawing, Third Period   93

Eileen Toomey
    Drag Race   94
    He Sleeps in My Room   95
    Dirty Water   96

Kimberly A. Collins
    Hand Me Down Mean   98
    Bessie's Men   99
    Paris Blues   100

Kate Hovey
    To Bluebeard   101
    Lilith Utters Ineffable Names   102

Pamela Gibbs Hirschler
    The Chibok Girls, One Year Later   103
    To Build a Universe   105
    Evangelical Admonition to a Young Girl   107

Mariel Masque
    Genesis   108
    Self Portrait   109
    Birth of a Poet   110

Lynn Valente
    I was a pencil   111
    Flute Player   112
    Literary Love   113

Sue Churchill
    I think of the Greeks 114
    Executive Order, January 2017 115

Ruth Mota
    Billie's Brazilian Ghost 116
    Brazilian Honeymoon 117
    Pechisso's Tale 118

Lynne McEniry
    poem 120
    If I were to die 121
    Summer Afternoon on Aquinnah Cliffs 122

Lynne Santy Tanner
    On this Bright Day 123
    Midsummer 124
    The Mocking Bird 125

Akua Lezli Hope
    Algeria 126
    Resurrections 127

Julie Rochlin
    Picking Peaches in the Dark 128
    Recuperation 129
    Camp Ontario, 1973 131

Joanne Godley
    Picnic 133
    Bois Caiman Ceremony 134
    Anatomy of a Scar 135

Virginia Bell
    The Skin Essay [excerpt] 136

Wendy Marie Vergoz
    His First Wife 142
    Popsicle 144

Bo Niles
    Why I believe in ghosts 146

    Topography   147

Arfah Daud
    Younger Days, Growing Up   148
    Will I Survive the Kitchen Sink   150
    Hooked   152

Tricia Coscia
    Rules of Engagement for Combat Robots   154
    Thakil   155
    Carrying to Term   156

Margie Shaheed
    LifeCycles   158
    WHEN WE GET TOGETHER   160
    Nostalgic Hair Affair   161

Gina Valdés
    Under the Eagle Sun   163
    A Brush Dipped in Night Ink   164
    Walking on Earth   165

Joanna Rose
    Apology to a Mother Long Dead   166
    Death School   167

Wendy Mitman Clarke
    Cold Front at Midnight   168
    Joe Pye Weed   169
    Note from the Tide, Falling   171

About the Poets   172

Notes   182

At the close of each poet's selection you'll find a statement by them that answers the question, "Why Poetry?"

50/50

Laura Apol

The Fox

> *What I thought I had left, I kept finding again*—W. S. Merwin

Is this how
she now comes to me—
a glimpse of tawny haunches,
dark muzzle and bright eyes?

The last time I saw her,
she had dyed her blond hair red.
It was brass-orange, a shade
she could not abide.

We washed it together,
my fingers pink with lather, the sink
filled with fuchsia suds.

~

This morning they gave me
five locks of her hair—amber lights,
copper, rose-gold.

I would have held her
had she let me
that desperate afternoon
—would have stroked her hair
until my hands were reddened
with blood.

And the fox? It crosses the road,
peers from the ditch. Turns away,
silent and wary—slips
into the merciless
weeds.

LAURA APOL

**INSTRUCTIONS FOR THE FRIENDS
WHO ARE SORTING MY DAUGHTER'S THINGS
THIS AFTERNOON**

Please keep in mind

I want her coats—the new one she got for skiing,
the old one she wore in the yard, the black one she wore
on the photo in the rain—and the green hat and scarf
she knitted in 6th grade. I want the games: Clue,
cribbage, backgammon, Trivial Pursuit. I want
the Rook cards, too. And any score sheets
with her name at the top. I want the pink hoodie
with the kangaroo, her yoga mat, all the unmatched
earrings she saved. I want her purses and belts,
her viola and her second-hand guitar. I want her
measuring spoons, her ironing board, the photo albums,
her last bottle of shampoo. I want the Birkenstocks
(even the ones with the worn footbeds;
especially the ones with the worn footbeds),
her picnic blanket, and all the yarn. Save her watercolors,
her great-grandmother's sewing machine, the t-shirts
she had set aside for a quilt, and her tent. I want her
pillow. Her stuffed elephants. Her felt-tipped pens.
The broken lamp in the shed she planned
to fix, the door knobs she replaced but never
threw out. Don't give away her nail polish
or her emery boards. Or any of her rings.
I want her hairbrush, the hair still caught in it.
Her toothbrush. Her last morning. I want the sun
in the window. I want the cats that woke and stretched
beside her. I want her last phone call, her choice.
Goddamn—what I want is her choice.

I spent ten years working in Rwanda, conducting workshops with genocide survivors using writing to facilitate healing. Then my daughter died - and everything I thought I knew about therapeutic writing was put to the test. For me, writing is the greatest source of healing I know, and now I can say it from the depths of my own grief: poetry is a means of survival; over and over, it saves me.

Pam Baggett

How Fathers Leave

Enraged. In love
with whiskey. With the lights
out, gun in hand.

With you cowering.
Two sisters, too.
Your mother in the chair
nearest the door.

Find her
by her voice:

This is ridiculous.

She flips the lights.
You hold held breath.
Your father in his underwear,
slumped on a kitchen stool.

She hustles you to bed.
A child, you sleep.

Wake, pack a pillowcase
of clothes, blanketful
of dolls. Startle at each
crackle after she tells you
his last words:

*If you're still here
when I get back from work,
I'll kill you.*

Kill the wife,
or kill the children, too?

With questions.
With no answers.
Fathers leave you
guessing when you go.

Pam Baggett

Remorse

While I slept, a trap snapped
on a mouse's neck in the kitchen.
For days, she'd strewn evidence
of her presence across the counters
and floor. Though I hid bread
and apples in the refrigerator,
cleaned up every crumb,
she lingered like a guest stranded
by cold, dodging the twelve-inch ruler
baited with peanut butter
and suspended over a garbage pail.
Disgusted, fearful of disease,
I set three guillotines.

The next morning, I found her:
eyes bulged from the blow,
a pool of blood at her mouth,
her pale upturned belly seeded
with small nipples. I flung
her body into the woods
for something hungry to find.

All that day I thought about her,
the small eager life drawn
by need to the pungent scent
of peanuts, the crush of tiny bones.

Why poetry? Why hard work that leaves you hungry, tired, tested, sated, elated?
One might as well ask, why sanity? Why joy?

Brenda Bell Brown

KEEP A MESSY HOUSE

keep a messy house
lose yourself in the haze-striated sheets of standing particles, fleek
shimmering bursts of dust floating down in glowing vertical lengthening sunlight
it is cinema seen between slit-eye pants of morning love
making dust bunnies mingle with puffs of bedding
moaning breaths of quicksilver hiding in the dark underneath
the bed, dust swirls
spewed forth by centrifugal force
escapees laughing in coupled tango through the opening of Mama's handmade coverlet
what happens to minutia when mixed up exponentially?
when gathered en masse tera over time
it becomes the outward shell of the scarab soul
loving the InnSæi
—the sea within

"dust from the foot of a generous woman, *Lord Krishna*, dust from her foot will cure you"
walk through my home and you will be saved from all ills
turn yourself into yourself
walk through
the sea within
and be soothed by life's art of noise

Brenda Bell Brown

We All Gots To Git

> *For some, home was close.*
> *For others, there was five hundred miles left.* —Michael Burkard, "The Sunday"

We.

Children crowded into Tong's after school for peppermint candy to stick inside giant dill pickles and stick-sticky orange pushups and crackly pig rinds fresh from the cooker down the street and and grape NeHi's, don't forget something to drink: *We thirsty!*

We.

Children hurried to finish summertime chores because Coach would not play you if you were late for practice to learn how to dribble, pitch, toss, palm, chunk, catch, shoot a pill, pigskin, softball, hardball, and tackle, strike, rush, slide, *Score!!!!* before the streetlights came on bright: *We home!*

We.

Children walked anywhere and everywhere in our neighborhood safe because each house, along the way, had eyes with nothing but love for us and kept vigil, for as longs as the world turned.

We.

Grown: weary to see our children suffer the cold while waiting to be bussed in the dead of winter.

Brenda Bell Brown

Sister. Girl. Don't you know, whole villages wake up from nightmares of your provincial puritanical dreams? You scheme to overturn wars rightly won by Brown babies faking dead on the highway [**#BLACKLIVESMATTER! #BLACKLIVESMATTER!**], screaming your way won't number their days in a world that was overcome a loooonnng time ago (don't you know?) way before greed pushed you who chose to sail the ocean blue to make gold the standard to weigh the wealth of the world and cut off Brown hands that traded it freely before you, the greedy, pilfered and pillaged their shores, then ya' blasted Black hands: trading diamonds for shackles, then ya' relegated to mines Yellow hands that spun silk for your insults and lies. Blow up! 'Cuz all these years, you never grew up to mature, only whine, baby, whine when your delicate sensibilities got teased by the mirth that your Dionysian ancestors coupled with fermented, mashed up, stank toe, grape juice in the first damn place. From it came mace to put down drunk crowds, impalement to root out sulfured hogs, tambourines to glory that were not keeping time to saints dancing but to the tone-deaf ancestors who top your malevolent strand who would deny mirth to Brown sisters only because they can. Ice queen, sit down and chill. Like the ghost town silicon made of the valley, don't you know that you are also obsolete? *Are we not women, and sisters?* Cheers.

—dedicated to the women thrown off the Napa Valley wine train for laughing-while-Black, 22 August 2015

Why poetry? my poetry: I will myself to write fast enough, stay awake long enough, go without food and still maintain my strength to scribe and tell all about You in the verse I will use to defy the quicken crystallized into sapphires and diamonds sparking deep down in Our ebony eyes; poetic truths, written in Your voice, reside long after We, the people, have passed on, spirit formed, into dawn. Asé

Christine Ernst

FOLD

there is a line   a long one
saturday at the P is a busy day
the P   or the V de P   or simply the Vatican
the saint vincent de paul society thrift shop on route 28
run by a catholic church   staffed mostly by old women
despite my rancor for the church I go almost every saturday   sometimes tuesdays too
for the thrill of the bargain
the hipness of upcycling   the stories in every cast-off
today is busy   everything is half off   so there's the line   in addition to which
the lady jamming things up today has a voucher
meaning she is in a pickle and received a voucher from the church aid society to shop here
most of us   us regulars   come here hunting for treasure   the cashmere scarf
the perfect chair for the guest room   the vintage table cloth   just last week I scored a brand new
bialetti moka pot and another cardigan I'll never wear
most of us shop here for fun
but the woman jamming up this line has a voucher   has a heap of stuff on the counter
mostly children's clothes   by the look of it she has at least an infant and a toddler and
a couple school-age kids
she has jeans and sweatshirts and pajamas and t-shirts and socks and onesies and coats and sweaters and sneakers and rainboots   also towels and two sheets and even
a brand-new-still-with-the-tags-on twin size star wars comforter with matching sham
Janet who is 83 is ringing each item in and Peg who is 87 if she's a day is folding and bagging   so slowly
taking time to exclaim over each thing *would you look at that hardly worn at all*   or   *isn't that precious?*
Janet holds up a tiny sweater and declares it a handknit   *you pay good money for that at a craft fair*   she says   so very slowly excruciatingly really the sale is rung in and bagged   with many pauses to check the total against the voucher to make sure she doesn't go over
the man next to me in line sighs loudly at regular intervals and people behind him grumble and shift in the way put-upon people in lines do   the inconvenience of it all you know   the guy next to me mumbles not out of earshot   *of course she has a voucher*   like poor people are the bane of his existence
like he himself is not waiting in line in a thrift shop to buy a used pair of swim trunks   and the woman ahead of me looks back at swim trunk dude and rolls her eyes in agreement with him   like this poor mother with a voucher is totally harshing her

saturday morning yard saling thrift-shopping chill
there is not a single thing for herself on the counter unless you count the threadbare mismatched towels
she is young   too young for four kids   thin   haggard   nails chewed to the cuticle   she looks anxious   harried   aware of the line behind her
aware of her voucher
but Janet and Peg are in no rush   if anything they slow down   folding everything just so   as if they know that no one takes time for this woman   all the kids' clothes are lovingly stowed in a gap shopping bag
all the linens into a ridiculous lily pulitzer tote   comforter in an oversized birthday gift bag like it's a present   they pamper her in a way only old catholic thrift shop ladies know   like they are packing her trousseau
her hope chest
they mutter over the total   checking and rechecking the number   and Janet announces at last that there is $1.75 left over   the line knows there is no cash back on vouchers and groans in unison   great she's gonna have to pick something else out   but Peg says *I know just the thing* and bustles out from behind the counter and into the shop   for 87 she's pretty fast   returns in a flash triumphant   with a dress
like a bridesmaid dress   a gown really   beautiful   deep pink   impractical   *this color is perfect for you*
Peg says   holds it up to the woman   and it is indeed perfect   *you would be so lovely in this*
like
Peg is fairy godmother and tonight is the ball
she tears the ten dollar ticket off the sleeve of the dress and gives Janet an even look *one seventy-five, Janet*   she says   Janet nods knowingly   like the nuns in the sound of music at the end when they take the distributor cap out of the nazis' car   *one dollar and seventy five cents* Janet says precisely as she peers through her readers and punches the numbers in
Peg folds the dress so carefully   and the line is mesmerized
one because it is a lesson in the dying art of ball gown folding
and two because it is an act of such tenderness
Peg cannot touch this woman   stroke her hair   hold her hand   tell her that in this moment she is cherished   but she can fold this lovely dress   so gently tucking the crinoline   folding the bow   smoothing the sleeves   she folds this dress like a sacrament   like jesus washing the feet of the disciples
there is a change in the line   a lightening
a silent cheer that the sale is almost complete for sure
but also a shift now for the woman   toward the woman   the line leans in a little   as if the dress   or   the gesture of the dress   the patient slow folding of the dress make eye rolling lady and swim trunk dude imagine the woman with the voucher as someone else
Janet and Peg finish the sale are all business again   they sign off on the voucher and

hand over the bags
she thanks them sheepishly and starts to leave   avoiding eye contact with the line behind her   Peg calls after her   *don't forget your star wars comforter! that's a prize!*   and leans over the counter with the last tote   the one that looks like a big present
she makes a joke
may the force be with you!   she calls
she has no idea

Christine Ernst

COGNATE MEANS BLOOD-RELATED

linguists have somehow identified a handful
of words that have survived since the last ice age
relics of a mother tongue spoken by hunter-gatherers somewhere
in neolithic anatolia
as the glaciers were receding 150 centuries ago
15,000 years of story and song and slang
millennia of uncountable
dialects in which we have misunderstood each other from the very beginning
the cognates of 23 proto-words persist
living fossilwords   or
ultraconserved as the archeolinguist
describes them:
spit   worm   flow   black   bark   ashes   hand   not   we
who   ye   that   pull   this
mother   man   old   fire   what   I   give   hear
and one word even more vigorous than the rest
the only word that occurs in some form in 700 living languages spanning
the families indoeuropean and chuk-chi-kam-chat-kan and
kartvelian   from the arctic to india   western china to ireland
spoken by half the people on earth for the past 15,000 years
one word distilled   the purest word   the absolute descendent of all words
the heir of language itself
thou
the word *thou*   and its living
cognates: you   tu   ti   turi   esh-te   te   t'kin   dhe   thou
thou   not *me* or *I* or even *we*   *thou*
the longing to be comprehended by the one not oneself contained inside the sound
thou   *dhe*   *t'kin*   *te*   *esh-te*   *turi*   *ti*   *tu*   *you*   *thou*
so that when I say
you! hear me, man! -- don't be a worm! pull your hand from the ashes and give this black bark to the old
mother — and no spitting in the fire!
I might be understood by a caveman in stone-age Turkey or a
reindeer herder in bronze-age Greenland   by a pilgrim at Stonehenge by
Alexander the Great himself   by anyone on
any number of continents tomorrow afternoon
understood through the ages in any language
the sounds I make familiar and eternal
but I am speaking to you   now
to you
you

Christine Ernst

CRADLE

so I'm reading about these baby sharks lately
baby sharks in big city aquarium tanks   only mother sharks   no father sharks in these tanks
holy smokes where did that baby shark come from   so I googled it and read also about
baby lizards baby snakes certain insects a few species of birds
all observed in captivity   so who the heck knows what's happening out in the wild
parthenogenesis   scientists call it
the phenomenon of virgin birth   spontaneous reproduction   occurring   when a species is
under profound environmental stress
now apart from the obvious implications regarding the necessity of father sharks
father lizards father snakes father insects fathers   and perhaps the y-chromosome in general
and with a nod to my catholic upbringing   lapsed and resentful as I am
I am wondering if anyone has considered the virgin mary in light of such science
since baby jesus was born at a time when his own species was under duress
and the virgin birth part   was the first piece of that fairy story   that sounded fishy to me so
what if
that bewildered girl in galilee in the cradle of civilization or hotbed of
intolerance and brutality   take your pick   what if poor unsuspecting mary
won our species' lottery   or simply drew the short straw   was chosen was
ordained by the principles of   darwinian evolution
was not exactly   visited   by the
angel gabriel though it is a lovely story
maybe mary the perpetual virgin was simply in the right place
at the right time or the wrongest time the catastrophic time
was charged by the universe and
parthenogenically conceived   or created   engendered   manifested   on her own
by herself   an answer to the maelstrom
magically birthed a savior at a time when humankind needed saving
(now we can never know the pillow talk in that bedroom in nazareth   but for the record   joseph
must have been a mensch)
but how ingenious that virgin mother how special that infant how unique and powerful that young man
to so   mostly posthumously   captivate the world
and the legacy of that thrall notwithstanding

for even jesus   that prince of peace   got co-opted by the haters
    are we   not   just last year next week this morning at 7:20   2000 or so years later
up the creek without a paddle   again   in catastrophic times
are we not seething as a species under profound distress   did I mention the haters
 and the rest of the   rutting   father shark hierarchy
are we not   then   by exquisite scientific extrapolation   by the miracle of chance
given the facts of population increase   and the intolerance and the brutality
and the global warming and the odds and the beautiful baby sharks abounding
given the well-documented ingenuity   of the queen of heaven herself
are we not here today   this minute   among the teeming masses
probably   hopefully   inevitably
surrounded by saviors?

Poetry is the most efficient way to distill and package and share the story. And the story—the telling, the receiving—will save us all.

Faith Paulsen

Poem in Response to Steve Nolan

> *I wanted to write a poem about a flower*
> *but the only flower I could bring myself to pen*
> *was the bloom of subcutaneous blood pooling*
> *around the neck of the Syrian man hanging*
> *in one of Assad's many underground prisons.* —Steve Nolan

Write about the violet blossoming
on the mother's cheekbone.
The bright anemone on the soldier's femoral artery.
On the migrant's dehydrated lips, a chrysanthemum.
On the young girl's headscarf, spatters of salvia splendens.
Compose a lyric about petals open-mouthed,
the tongue-like stamens.
Fall like a bee into the throat of the iris,
the scent that gushes
like a scream,
pollen coating every surface.
The snowdrop faces of children choking on sarin gas.
Write a poem about the backhoe shoveling life-vests
like yellow tulips,
the still life skin of the drowned toddler, a white rose.
Write about the field of poppies.

Faith Paulsen

Venus

> *These carvings are the oldest figurative works of art made by Homo Sapiens, and they are known collectively as Venus figurines.*—Judith Thurman, "Ur-Mothers," The New Yorker

But I imagine
someone sitting cross-legged
on the dry plain
a flint axe in one hand
an oval shaped stone in the other
chipping form into the roundness
carving thin braceletted arms
limestone fingers pressing
into breasts engorged with milk.
The sharp edge of the tool
bores clefts on knees,
the dark cave of the navel.
For the sides of the nose,
lines are scored.
Then lidded eyes, rosettes
of braided hair.
In her warm palm,
the image is sanded and polished.
She dusts it with ochre—
a gift, a self-portrait
for her daughter.

Because I wrote a novel that wanted to be poetry. Because my Master's thesis was two thousand words for "Wow." Because my first language is metaphor. Because the only way to say what I want to say is to say it slant. Because the rivers clap their hands and like a diamond in the sky, because of sidewalks, ocean waves, and birdsong. Because words, because breath.

Tori Grant Welhouse

Three poems from
**LUNCH
A P r i m e r
in Poems Stashed**

(in My Daughter's Lunchbox Her Last Year
Before Going Away to College)

Lesson Eighteen.

Intuition

Telescoping from your cervical spine
in a barbed coatrack.

Frequency in your fingers,
depths of your clearie eyes,

you develop a signal
to your satellite self.

Wiseness is recognizing pattern.
Repeating waves of sound, light

reflect an inner tower.
You learn to detect the jerk

of dishonesty, the disingenuous,
the velocity of a lie.

Tori Grant Welhouse

Lesson Twenty-One.

Sex

One side of it
a screaming,
teeth at your neck,
swing of the hammerblow,
blunting the soft
bolster of the body,
spine trilling,
marimba wood
malleted fiercely.

The other a flickering
tongue-lick flame,
melting coins of butter
in your belly-button.
You will be candlewicked
by two fingers
and spit.

TORI GRANT WELHOUSE

LESSON TWENTY-TWO.

Solitude

You give yourself room,
susceptible to plushness, very fine hairs.
You're not wrong, not right,
benign as a window, cool, glass pane,
relishing flatness, passivity.

You sit bowl, slurp yourself,
a satiation of hunger, thirst, peace.
You might hold a teacup, fingering
the glaze of it between your blessings.

Free from the ricochet of other people,
bothersome mouth-breathing,
exactingness of places. Your spleen,
or other inexplicable organ,
happiest when left alone.

My *manifesto* has always been these lines from Erica Jong: "If a woman wants to be a poet, she must dwell in the house of the tomato." Poetry is a call to live a thin-skinned life. To care. To contribute. To corroborate all that we are in our houses of tomato—our beautiful, wonderful, and aggravating differences. And our very similar yearnings.

Amy Small-McKinney

Poem Beginning with a Line by Daisy Zamora

I am looking for the women of my house.
I am looking for them under my bed
where they live to evaluate my thighs.
Look for them when they take off their pearls
before falling asleep.
I remember them as tendrils of hair.
I did not know them very well.

I wanted to sail to a new country, learn to shoe horses. Or live
in a desert where water drains from a sea, then loosens from its salt.
I wanted to return to modern Russia, mark out designs for tin tea kettles.
Or swim below with a dolphin close enough to read its tag. I did not want
to sleep the day away. I did not want to be a faux fur coat. I did not want.

I wanted to be the girl who could lift houses,
solved mysteries with a flashlight.
I hung a poster of a woman murdered for refusing,
traveled to Odessa to look for a grandmother who argued for Trotsky, then changed her
         mind.

I change my mind,
bring them out from under my bed.
They are smaller than I imagined.
They are breakable as saucers.
I tell them I love them anyway,
tell them their pearls are teeth that can cut
into my nightmares.
I tell them I am skydiving.
I sail slowly down toward the body I am learning to love.
I show them my body with its scars.
I show them my daughter, there she is, I say, she of our house.

Amy Small-McKinney

In Our World

I scrape on a window, I have a beak,
no feathers.
I cannot remember my life.

Are there trees? I believe one.
A red maple. And a road stretching

beyond a pond. To pass, one needs identification.
I am not a refugee   unidentified.
I am not homeless   a bed.

I am lost—

                Cannot find—
        We cannot find.

      We are floor of glass.
            Wall of Babel.

I scrape against rock and the world's hubris,
its rough skin.
Sandpaper, I am sand and paper.
Only the floor, glass.

I cannot find my voice. Beak against stone.
This is not a bird, no flight.

Amy Small-McKinney

Treatment for Panic, Low Grade and Chronic

Place your body into a bathtub
without water. In place of water
allow a small tree to join you.
It must not be a willow. Avoid
the dwarf cherry. It is sweet
but needs care. I suggest a *Gleditsia
Triacanthos* commonly known as Honey
Locust. You may eat its pulp, and
at the very least something that won't weep.
There may not be enough room for both of you.
You must choose.

Because it is breathing. Because it is a limb, inseparable from my body. Because without it, there is no world that makes sense. Because its language and its form are the materials of a most beautiful vase that expands and narrows as needed and always the safest container for chaos. Because I have been writing since a small girl and cannot stop. Because poetry is both silence of the self and embrace of community.

Mary Catherine Loving

Regarding my actions over the past week

After we decided to end it all, once and for all,
I rushed straight away into the bellies of my aunties,
and we, we did what we witches are wont to do:
we stitched our enemies' lies into a fortress
against the coming winter, seeded the clouds
with our lovers' names, rubbed sage

onto our rounding bellies, then
swung low to balance the Earth's turning.
Enlightened, a few of the younger ones among us
conjured ghosts to frighten strangers—
But you should know:
(and my eyes narrow as I write this)

We are not afraid.
It is no longer dark where we live
in this damp place between then and now.
Between once and never
we take to craft: take to the taking back
of name, stem and purpose—take to the

creation of singular moments, moments
designed to warn fickle lovers, designed to capture
cold hearts. Scare doubters into belief.
(But, we have never doubted. We have always believed.)
After you decided enough was too much,
I rushed

straight away into the bellies of my mothers
wallowed there in the wonder of it all,
and we, we witches
thought about calling nine, one, one,
instead
we did what we witches are wont to do:

we drank our pee,
filled cauldrons with our fetid laughter,
stuffed our hearts until they suffered

stuffed our hearts
until those beating, beating rhythms
confessed their inability to lead us:

they could only follow. Ah, in those final moments
we witches burned lies into fodder.
Who could dare expect less than these things—
cauldrons. hearts. lies. laughter.
    But look: nary a one drowned in her own tears.
    Not a single one stumbled over *what if*.

Mary Catherine Loving

A Slave Woman Recalls the Affair

I keep three wishes read:

        I

To shed myth written on this black skin,
to erase History's often-repeated tale
and spin anew: a telling that bears no trace of the old.

        II

To be done with speculation: his wanting
known early to me, given breath in each command.
Punishment meted, unequal, unkind—his kingdom,
once impoverished, reborn. My name
sullied in old wives' tales.

        III

To shake self loose from remembrance.
These three.

Mary Catherine Loving

Interplanetary Love Jones

It is not the Earth's rotation that unsettles me. No.
It is the rush, and the rugged, full drop, then
juggling my bruised emotions as I teeter face-first into Mars
that drives me off balance. Heartbreak? Perhaps.
Certainly.

But even heartbreak
can not begin to account for my unsteadiness
of balance. Of vision. Cannot begin to explain
my need for camphor. And bandages.
Lots of bandages.

Each time I leave Earth spinning in my rear view,
each time I shuck-and-jive to Jupiter's metronome
or coordinate my hula in time to Saturn's moons

I must recalibrate. Piece-meal my way
back from deepest,
darkest space
without help from astronauts, Pluto,
or God—

(this comes from one who claims no religion
no master except Lord Buddha in times of imminent crisis)

And without empathy from any one of you.

So to steady myself I wrangle stars from the big dipper,
then spin them 'round and 'round on a sunbeam
until the dizziness fades.

(The dizziness, I insist, will surely fade).

Most certainly not the Earth's rotation
that sets my fanatic's heart aflutter. No.
It is the pull of Mercury's
scary magic; his physical self
flailing,

then adjusting my fall.
Again. And again.
A galaxy of errors performed. For me.
Near me. Frighteningly
near me.

What?

No. Venus most certainly is not the answer.
She has delivered unfaithfulness a hundred times or more.

Poetry because it makes me whole again. Poetry creates boundaries around those things that my disability will not permit me to do for myself alone and highlights new ways, new approaches for me to try. Poetry because it teaches me again and again that words matter; words are my strength, my rock. Poetry because it challenges me to write about those things I shunned in another life. Another age. Poetry. Because.

JC Miller

X

1/

Bring your hands from heaven
and seven candlesticks. Answer
my knocking call. Banish the crumbling
drumbeat of walls, the X
the building inspector traces on my door.

2/

I am vine that prays for you
as prey. Take me
from what is gravity fed.
I want the friction pulley of your hands
to hoist me as herons fly.

3/

I long for your touch to tanager me
blue and yellow, to shape-shift us
as cloud what love owes and needs.
I recommend me, dear husband.

4/

Together, in the palace of sun,
let us tapestry its golden fields
as shadow does. Where air is country,
I will be orchid field in your hands,
fire-crowned, windblown.

5/

My heart is a kite
locked in dark bituminous as oil.
My knotted streamer olivines, massing
as after a disaster
at light chinking the door.

JC Miller

To My Husband & Other Strangers

Forgive me tomorrow I cannot
remember your name. I call
you what identity
a different mother gave her son.

I am not a bad person but fear
and forgetting are so close. Remember
the times mothers sometimes
had to backhand them apart.

Now my mind cannot stream
letters to mouth, the pause
longer and my anger, too.
Remember that woman painting
mystery smile I demanded last week,
the road what it is
leads to my father's house.

Yesterday, it was dandelion
and the act of blowing
on my hand brought me back
lying on spiked Bermuda grass,
the sky so endless untroubled
as the seeds tumbled like little
gymnasts, like skydivers, brave.

Today I reached in my cupboard for the word
for the red stuff I put on your home fries
and eggs. My clock
is melting. Salt on the glass edge,
before that sweet drink, such
a bitter taste.

JC Miller

Honey the Air

Glory the days the earth so green everything
grows lucky. Dogs leaping, climb
the air's invisible wall. What joy all things
strive for! Cherry blossoms bud
my hair young. Willows fashion the wind.
New-eared boxwoods glisten
as grass snakes stir in cursive. In soupy mud,
shallow-rooted trees upend where earthworms shrug.
Unhitched hawks pivot, each thermal a slope
between glides they swerve.
Sing praise, swallow gutter-perched. Burst lark
into aria. Ridged in swamps, snapping turtles
flood a grin. But bees that honey the air,
where do they shiver now?
Blossoms, shake the dew for them.

Poetry lets me travel with words. Sometimes, poetry is my stubborn sister who refuses to comply, sometimes a ghost, sometimes a companion.

Nan Becker

Suddenly, and then suddenly, the drought river unhides
a riparian pool—the water left lay as polished stone.
A young grey swan efforts through its solitaire—light

darkens, and the mirage colts like a penance. Across,
the trees blink the same view up or down. Gulls glide
in spirals—herons, cautiously gluttonous, step over new

bounty scattle-ing between their toes. Up ahead, three
deer plea where once they drank. In the river remains, fish
crowd closer their single lives with the blank misgivings

of a half-blind horse riding too close to the wall. All its
solicitudes lie in these forwarding waters pressed by winds
the day leans into. Only we are surprised by surprise,

our minutia, the circumstances of life, of memories' life
—what you never received and gave up asking for, all that
lacking, insistent as that young swan's hunger.

Nan Becker

The color lent by the sky and the cupping river banks
was penciled by a small life passengering across like a tear
in the steady pace of a sleeper's heart.

What home here is not there? What is it it must outwit?
Or is its arable so without bound —like the wings of a red tail,
splayed taut in a rise, rising beyond reason or use.

As if water would beat a heart or air breathe, their acuity
blind to the margins of *here* and *there*— what it means
to be *more*. Is this affection and also, its glove unrequited

—for what was ever said between us outside of necessity?
Still, I was dazzled by what I heard. I heard rain falling
to its reaches, I heard the ground swell.

I don't have a statement—all my considerations are in the poems. I think we are all asking the same unanswerable questions.

Gail Langstroth

Number 2, Manhattan-bound Bronx train

No earbuds or phone—
she sings sweet & natural
nobody has to know.

The slow pitch rises
sinks on the word:
no – ooo – o—ow.

Her extra-long nails, decaled, white,
pink, dots, sparkles, striped hearts—tap the beat,
then rest on the zipper-ribbed curve of her purse.

nobody has to know
*I can – oh I can
oh – oh oh oh—.*

Our train leaves bright Bronx sun,
dives into the dark & dirt
of tunneled underground.

"This is the number 2, Manhattan-bound
express train, next stop—"
nobody asked to know.

In front of us a cool guy with unblemished,
very cherry red high-tops: like hot,
like heat for icy NY streets.

I return to my muse—
the magnificent twists of her vine-y hoop earrings
brush the cowl neck of her sweater.

*I can – oh I can—
and you—
nobody asked to know.*

I listen, but can't tell,
asked or *has*—doesn't matter,

her lyrics lift stale train air,

make it brilliant like the sun
I know is there/outside.
She sings it like I feel it:

happy this morning/today happy
like in love happy &
nobody has to know.

My train thoughts fill with future.
What brings this lift?
What leads to Broadway & W. 110th?

"Stand clear of the closing doors."
On my way to visit Jean
I step onto the street.

A squished
Cheetos bag
salutes spring, glistens

orange with sun.
This day is my beloved, &
nobody has to know.

Gail Langstroth

Negative Incursions: Rula Halawani's Photograph

This is not:
woman clothed with the sun.

This is:
I know end.
I know explode.

Stripped to moon
steel pounds incessant staccato.
I know mercury/dead.

I stand fallen freeze glow after
what left has left
after night after night terror

rips shredded from dream from stench
from cup from wall whether
I want to or not—

I see with my mouth:

my shut/white
barb-eyed
star.

Gail Langstroth

The Farmhand Lost His Voice

When you say *voice*,
is it a sound, or the graffiti hearts
I saw on a cold wall this morning?

Doesn't a saw
have a voice when it rips the trunk
and shreds the frozen air?

Is voice the force that seeks?
Unshaped breath rolled on a tongue
through teeth/lips?

Blood split to a dripping stop.

The farmhand lost his voice
as he watched his African brothers being sliced
to pieces. He couldn't scream.

As a eurythmy performer, I experience how words, sounds, and what we work with in the making of poems, are vital substances. These substances pertain to the very essence of who we are as human beings. When I attempt to translate a thought or feeling into language, when I am in the art of poem-making—I enter the pulse of this mystery.

Rose M. Smith

Blood from the Son

> *after announcement of no charges for Dontre Hamilton,*
> *a schizophrenic young man shot 14 times*
> *in Milwaukee, Wisconsin and no charges for his death,*
> *—December, 2014*

They think 'cause you quiet you say, *Okay*.
Okay to the raised hand, *okay* to the hard word
flung from uniformed tongue, til the dam of your brain
overflows with words. Through current and weed,
cast-off scales, the ghosts of dead boys reeking
with the cold breath of gladiolas, the cold words come.
A bright cascade of rainbows flows
past your pent up sound, your curled-back fist,
hands balled against the scrambled lash of language
that beat you long ago into submission.

You were once the absent word, the nothing felt.
You were the nothing thought right, nothing said right.
What now of that startled lad within you,
the one once taught to cower?
From where comes this man who pulls your reins
to turn you, away from *Run*, away from the fear
that striped your back, muddied your thoughts,
back to meet your torment at its face?
Your were the nothing felt that was real
within your private storm. How present now
the misplaced torment even drugs can't help explain.

After fourteen points of unleashed rage,
blood from the son I will never have
cries out with yours from the ground at Red Arrow Park,
a son's life soaking into fallow ground, fear a river
roiling in the blades. Blood that will never carry
air to your schizophrenic lung. Your beached fish
flutter not enough to put an officer at ease.
You slept without class on a wooden bench.
Lay too long in public view. Looked too scary.
Looked too black, too little like a Starbucks groupie

one time too many, two, then three. Then fourteen.

Even a wild cat, cornered, roars into a predator face,
lets out its claws to tear leathered skin,
life-bearing flesh, to take the muscled arm of that attack
into its mouth. Holds on fast even as its own bones break.
Blood from the mouth defeated pours onto sallow ground.
There are more than fourteen small drops here.
How do I get my young man's shed blood back?

Rose M. Smith

Mourning Season

If you ask, she will tell you first
how missing the light shuffle of his feet
in the hardwood hallway yawned inside her
like three hours past hunger,
will tell you how many corners
have since grown grey, shrouded
by the hard work of daddy long legs
in cellar roof beams, in unstirred edges
of the Florida room she does not sit in anymore,
and how the woods beyond the back fence
lost their symmetry beneath dead branches
blown to ground by Hurricane Ike
when it bullied its way up past Louisiana
the same year he went missing, in the Spring,
in the night, in the storm. She will not tell you
she cried when the papers came. Once.

She will call him the ache in her back, cold
chill in the room when everyone else complains
it is too warm. That sometimes he is fever,
a deep sore festering in soft brain matter.
He is myrrh, a bitter belly she tries to kill
with Coke or Killians, to belch out angst
that weighs upon her like costume crystal earrings
suspended on a chain—light enough to bear,
constant enough to tear through tender flesh
unguarded. She will say she hates mowing
grass on the yard's deep slope, has conquered
plumbing, paint, has stripped the carpet from
the front room that he loved, replaced the fence
he had promised to for years, rooted up
each shrub that usurped the ones she'd wanted.
She will say she is fine, loves being without
answering to. Her eyes are dry.
These days, her eyes are dry.

Rose M. Smith

TAKE

have daughter.
have daughter, have love gift.
have daughter, lose powerless,
    have beauty, have reason, have life.
        have joy. have purpose, have universe. have *protect*.
     have nurture, have feed, have *protect*.
have home, have cradle, have neighbor.
neighbor says *hi*, says *friend*.
neighbor says... neighbor what? neighbor run.
neighbor say man take. neighbor say man take daughter.
neighbor say man take.
man take? man take? can't lose.
lose daughter, lose self.
lose daughter, lose power, lose universe.
lose caution. lose *hold back*, lose *stop*, lose pain.
      lose time. go. that way. neighbor say
                  man take daughter that way.
lose slow. lose sore knee, lose pain, lose fear, just go.
neighbor say man take treasure. lose caution, hear scream. chase.
chase man chase scream. chase *danger* chase scream chase *man* chase scream chase daughter chase—scream! *daughter scream* chase *hard* chase *bastard* chase *universe* chase *jesus, don't let him!* chase *jesus!* chase already jesus running chase scream chase scream chase angry chase man. find angry find man. find man. find man. find man on daughter—*angry*. chase fearless. chase fearless. *pull*. pull man off daughter find angry lose pull back lose caution lose holy make fist. make fist fly. make man know. make man know you don't take daughter you don't hurt daughter you bastard you freak you son of a bitch you shit. you freaking fuck my daughter you ... whimper. take daughter. take boot. take… angry. take boot. take wish i had something, i'd... take boot. take boot. take… hold tighter daughter. still angry still angry, take boot. take daughter. *take* daughter, *take* daughter. take daughter take *sweet jesus* take *sweet*... take *breathe*. hold daughter, take *breathe*. take *breathe*. dial 9-1-1 tell come tell come take *breathe*. hold daughter take *breathe*. take bleeding. take so much blood take *hurry man bleeding man bleeding!* take *breathe*. take careful. take sharp pain take breath take breath take man still bleeding take *breathe*. man still bleeding man bleeding *oh god man bleeding* take *breathe*. man bleeding, no breath. man still bleeding, no breath. take daughter. take time. take *daughter*. take *universe*, hold *universe*, breathe, take time. take

life. take daughter? *take that*. take life. take daughter. take daughter *home*. take nothing back. take nothing back. take nothing back.   take   back   *nothing*.

I am a consummate introvert. Making small talk in a room full of strangers—definitely not my strong suit. But poetry makes me do things I would not otherwise do: Stand at a microphone in front of ten or in front of hundreds to give the poem its best life. Poetry is the release valve on my life, its shared remains the identity by which I am known of others.

Janet MacFadyen

After

From the caverns of my lungs
I breathe out mist, take cloud

for a dress, stand straight
as the woman on top of a column,
      a jug of olive oil
           balanced on her head.

I could walk in the midst
of waters, throw off the clothes

of the man who raped me, don
      these blown feathers, bones
           of seabirds.

I pull
a scrap of silk
through the hollow of a flute,
      I swab my breath.

Grass grows, the corn grows.

      My true body underneath
      almost fills its cocoon.

Janet MacFadyen

Feeding the Peat Stove

O valve of my heart,
firebox, ash tray, ash bucket.
Essence of peat, plant matter, bone.

Everything incinerates
into a smoky pitchyness so thick
it comes off on the fingers.

This is how I heat the body and hearth,
nurse the smoldering like a baby, feed it
or it dies.

      It has a great
saltiness to it, like blood, is a slow grieving
for all my attempts at mothering, my frantic kitchenry,
the saucepans and clattering.

If there is
no nourishment, if the stove
neither heats nor cooks, then hunger

boils the pot and the belly runs amok,
the belly is the smelter that stirs and frets
and finally ignites.

      I have done it again—
set the house on fire with cold and neglect,
wrapped the fire blanket around and around
myself, my children—

    O this good house
turned inside out,
these hungry children, my good intentions.

Where is the cook?
Whose hand on the ladle?
Who feeds this child
      who is myself?

Janet MacFadyen

When I Understood

how fast the life could flow
I held on to myself, then reached for you.
We flew hand in hand
over dark streets and city blocks,
the park with its nighttime maples, the fields laid low
by the deep hand of soil—
How could we know what was coming?
The branches budded, the buds leafed out,
leaves exploded into summer, and fall
tumbled golden over our shoulders.

We could be beings cloaked in gold.
We could be arrayed in fur, the nose
leading ours lives forward.
Into the surging wind we cried
Come on, come on but we could not see
what the future beheld in its compound insect eye.
It was enough to breathe: this, then this.
I embrace myself. I reach for you.

There, there.
There, there.

Poetry is a restorative function for me, connected with sleep, with evolving. Often I'm processing something I experienced years ago, some landscape I never understood. I like my poems to be journeys, and if the journey is through a surreal or archetypal landscape, I like to look around and learn from it. Then I have other poems that are simply visceral; they start in the ground and end in the kitchen, often involving root vegetables.

Ruth Goring

CANCIONCITAS DE REMIENDAS

Cantas lo inesperado
desde el buque donde cuelga
la bandera del estirado mar,
desde el estuche de hierbas,
la limpieza de aguas
a veces suave y otras tormentosa.

Tus labios aprenden
esta pared de tapia
que rodea tu aterrizaje.
Las hojas son lenguas
agitando incansables
loores al viento,
un pentecostés de clorofila
rezando *perdón, perdón*.

Algo surge en tu sueño
como bufanda levantada en brisa,
el secreto que guardabas
se abre, pequeño sol,
yema dorada y perfecta.
Te levantas cambiada.

Y aquí, aquí sigues
caminando, y camina lluvia,
los puños gigantescos de las nubes,
andas mojándote,
bofeteada. Cómo cansa
el olor a tierra y pavimento
mojado, invierno alargado,
la devoltura de carbon
a calentamiento a hielo
derritido en los polos
al reboso de los mares
a estas gotas: llanto

y necesidad. Tu cabeza,
tus hombros cargan justa

SMALL SONGS FOR MENDING

You sing the unexpected
from this boat with its banner
of the spreading sea,
from the purse of grasses,
the cleansing of waters
now gentle, now a storm.

Your lips are learning
this adobe wall
that surrounds your landing.
The leaves are tongues
tirelessly waving
praises to the wind,
a pentecost of chlorophyll
chanting *forgive, forgive*.

Something surges in your sleep
like a wind-flurried scarf,
the secret that you harbored
opens, a small sun,
perfect golden yoke.
You arise changed.

And you go on
walking, here, and rain walks too,
the clouds with their great fists;
you walk drenched,
buffeted. How it wears on us,
smell of wet earth and pavement,
this long season of rain,
the shifting of carbon
to burning to ice
melted at the poles
to overflowing oceans
to these drops: need

and weeping. Your head,
your shoulders carry this

ansiedad, aquí. Y camina

la historia, llevándonos
desde atrás, mansos y rebeldes
igualmente bofeteados.

Y tú, cambiada, caminando
la tierra que no cambias
con su llanto y sus fragancias,
sus ramos de jacaranda,
tacana de la selva
alzando copas suculentas
a las mariposas
que se levantan blancas
y azules como pétalos del cielo,

cargando su propia historia
liviana y grácil,
señales que susurran
en todo momento: *por favor,
por favor.*

reasonable worry, here. And history

walks, herding us
from behind, the meek and the resisters
buffeted alike.

And you, changed, still walk
the earth you cannot alter
with its lament, its fragrances,
its jacaranda branches,
rainforest heliconia
lifting succulent cups
to butterflies that rise
and fall like white
and blue like petals of the sky,

carrying their own light
and graceful history,
signs that without ceasing
breathe *please, if you
would be so kind.*

Ruth Goring

The run-on sentences of Saramago

draw a calm breathlessness
    across pages,

are a wind,
    a long rope,

tread the worn path of sayings,
    The work of the child is small
    but the one who disdains it will fall,

they are pinned with rare knots,
    comma-looped and rich with voices,

they gesture in fitful dreams,
    assert authority,

climb massive ladders of thought,
    guide us in blindness.

The worst blind man is the one
    who does not want to see.

I labyrinth, I center,
    lapped by brushstrokes,

consciousness, I say
    we are all woven,

a rough wool,
    the blindness binds us,

Saramago traces our path,
    looser than stitching,

we tangle and snap free,
    the sentences of Saramago

are a whip,
    are a great tenderness.

Ruth Goring

Message

There was something important
for me to say, but then came the water
in which I waded a bright shore,
then came the regal August sky
and the table work for my hands with glue
at first and many kinds of paper
especially the fire-colored paper
and the cunning buttons and words
crouched to spring, and so much
along the rims, and this
is what I always wanted, things
to make, so later in the kitchen,
white beans with apricots and cardamom
and ginger over rice. So these
are all I have to tell you, and the fire,
the blue along its long night edge.

Research shows that we tend to grow happier as we grow older. That certainly holds true for me, in a complex way. Writing poetry brings me joy, but much of the time it's so dang hard. The words do not fly onto the page; they seep reluctantly or surge in messy clumps. Often I would rather do almost anything else. Then, sometimes, they speak back to me and I remember why I am alive.

Helena Kim

Field of Possibility

Up on the hills of *Kokoiki*, 'Red Star'
in the field of possibility,
Mercury runs across the grass, his tail in the wind.
Golden light washes over waves of green.

I lean against mossy rocks
and touch my tender heart.
The wind echoes through the ironwoods,
brings me to that space in between
the sounds.

Tibetan Buddhist monks garbed
in crimson and orange appear in the field.
Hundreds of them prostrate towards me.
In absolute awe, I bow to the ground.

My heart cracks open to earth, trees
and sky where egrets cross
the clouds into the blue.
I hear, "You are on your path of light,
however impossible it seems."

Tears well up from the unseen corners in me,
flow downward, wash away the past.
Mercury comes, leans close,
and we watch the spirits leave.

In their wake
blue dragonflies circle around us
dip their transparent wings in the light.

Helena Kim

Pele's Fire

Born of water and earth
I bow to the sweeping ocean below the cliffs
my head touches the saltlicks on red earth
sky touches my back.

Again I am out here at the edge
beyond the field of tall grass
and the cows grazing below trees.
Sun blazes over the archipelago of the Hawaiian Islands
born of water and fire.

I breathe in the ocean, its metallic salty air.
September, the warmest month reminds me of
walking down the boardwalk at Asbury Park
listening to Springsteen's "Jersey Girl" blaring.
Looking past the people suspended in the summer scene
and the dark blue Atlantic Ocean, I felt
someone was waiting for me beyond the horizon.

Here I am, thirty years later
in the same body but no longer a familiar self,
I call in the elements and directions.
I am the Korean shaman dancing wildly in my vision
spinning away layer after layer, until
Korea, Jersey, Seattle are gone. Until
even the haphazard and precious lovers of my past have melted. Until
even the familiar songs from my youth have evaporated.

There
in the core
I am light born out of darkness—
Pele's Fire.

Helena Kim

Paper Shirt, Paper Pants

Paper shirt and paper pants we used to fold
two oceans away and four decades ago
on that shiny enameled floor in our home in Seoul.
The three of us huddled on the floor
or was it all the sisters? Four of us
learning from an auntie this small way
of containing our emotions.

Folding and straightening the lines
refolding into smaller squares
until that empty piece of paper shaped into a shirt
another, puffy legged pants.
Tucked into one another they were complete
keeping our hearts from spreading
into the wide open space of Mother's sad silence.

Poetry encapsulates for me—moments of being—in the most succinct, profound, and poignant expressions. While I was recovering from a serious illness, I could assign meaning to the devastating experience through metaphors, similes, and imageries, with rhythm and cadence. Writing poetry gave me a perspective that helped me move from the deepest darkness into the light.

Phyllis Price

The Shepherd's Wife

One grandfather kept sheep, walked fence lines at dawn
counting heads—stench of wool wet from night rain

a primal perfume to his nose most would not understand.
In late spring he rounded the herd for shearing,

freed them of binding habits like nuns after Vatican II.
Grandmother cautions: *Careful not to nick them.*

I don't want the stain of blood on wool
so deep that I can't work it.

Phyllis Price

Mesa Dreams

after O'Keeffe's New Mexico

How did New York hold you
all those years—

by some dark seduction
of architecture,

romance of angle and curve,
opposite attraction,

the thrill of intersection,
fingernails of wind

on towering walls,
monoliths you captured

on canvas, redemption of blue sky
above the gloom?

Was it such as these, or was it Stieglitz—
big mustache and glass plate camera—

his world black and white,
contrast and texture,

yours a cappella, as poignant,
as true as hollow bone?

Phyllis Price

Blessing of the Old Horse

After the funeral, I take the long way home.
Indigo shadows drape the Blue Ridge.
Somber adagios play on NPR.
Around a curve in the familiar road
I see the old white horse working the fence line
in search of green pasture.
I ease the car onto the shoulder and get out.

Raising her head mid-chew, she looks at me
with knowing eyes, saunters over to offer
the worn suede of her nose.
I lean in close to her warm breath,
tiny hairs on her muzzle brush my cheek,
pulling me into the present, grounding me
from the terrible flight of three white doves
released to signify the spirit of a friend,
soaring, unbridled at last.

Poetry because poems are tiny stories I can tell no other way. Poetry because of the brevity, the sheer tenacity of its sparseness. Poetry because the writer can celebrate, remember, find peace, trouble the water, heal old wounds, experience re-birth, and give as much to the reader. Why poetry—for the mysterious joy of it!

NADINE PINEDE

NOTE TO SELF

When life's hurricane
comes bearing down
threatening to
lash you senseless,
seek shelter.
Find the warm
blanket you caress
like the felted fur
of your cat
curled before
a glowing hearth,
of breath that fills
both heart and earth.
Breathe.
There's always time
to curse the darkness.
After the tears,
light a honeycomb candle
and heal your own sun.
The bridge
from sorrow to joy
may seem to vanish
in the flood,
but who says you
can't join those
who cross over,
with a single
braided rope
of gratitude.

Nadine Pinede

Water Bearers: Summer 2016

For Ieshia, Tess & Michelle

How you stood firm,
your bare arms extended
in your soft summer dress
to the riot police,
looking beyond them
to the promised land
where all lives matter,
and your son will not die
at the hands of those
meant to protect us
on a cracked asphalt highway,
your serenity shone.

How you walked steady,
your small fist raised
against the anger of 300,
whose black boots
kick refugees and migrants,
and anyone else they say
should never belong,
boots that shake cobblestone
and wake up the dead
who beg us
to never forget,
you faced all of this with
your courage alone.

How you spoke truth,
your bold voice roiling
at seeing your daughters,
their faces pressed to the glass
as they left for school
with armed guards
"What have we done?"
All the sacrifice, insults,
the most death threats endured

so The House
built by slaves
could become yours
one we could all call our own,
a promise in place.

How well we know
wildfire hate
that leaps parched hills,
and sears the heart
to ash—yet still
you bear water
with the balm of your grace.

NADINE PINEDE

STONES IN THE SUN

He threw stones
from up above
from a higher plateau,
in the shadow of the temple.

He threw stones.
There were two, the younger one, beer in hand,
asked in English
"Is this the path to the pyramid?"

He threw stones.
Something didn't feel right
in my gut
that primordial fissure of fear.

He threw stones.
A young couple from the village
walking hand-in-hand, made a sudden U-turn.
I should have asked why, instead of starting the climb.

He threw stones.
Fight, flee, or freeze.
Which would you have chosen?
I did all three, in reverse.

He threw stones.
The older one, tall and silent, wagged his finger
and bent down.
Only then did I turn and run.

He threw stones.
Next to me my ancestors ran,
the way they ran from slave catchers
the way they ran to freedom
together on crooked ground
stone shower hailing down.
At the bottom of the mountain
where rock slabs met the earth

I fell.
On my hands and knees
bleeding, earth caked hair
I wanted to turn back
and ask, *Why?*

He threw stones.
Inside I shook my fist in anger. Denied my pilgrimage.
I wanted to see the pyramid
and the petroglyphs inside the temple shrine.

He threw stones.
Sticks and stones
may break my bones,
but *why* will always haunt me.
Did it matter
that I was an immigrant
to a nation whose leader
threw stones of his own?

He threw stones.

In the beginning was the stone.
Space rocks exploded
to rip a veil of stars.
Two hundred million years ago,
Pangaea broke apart
to separate the oceans.
We emerged from black water
blinked in savannah sun
we children of Lucy,
stone in hand
to kill what we ate,
and each other.
We lived the Stone Age
some of us carving and painting
by firelight in caves.

The Taïno came by sea,
from what would later be Mexico.
They named their island Ayiti,
the Land of High Mountains.

They carved their petroglyphs
before doom arrived (cloaked in amity)
before the poet warrior Anacaona
led the resistance. Captured by the Spanish,
Golden Flower chose to die
rather than live as their concubine.
Taíno survivors, bleeding and scarred,
fled up the mountains
and bound their fate with escaped slaves,
whose welted backs
were a geography of pain,
and whose gods dwelled in waterfalls.
Together they created my ancestors,
my grandmother who sent me Unity's *Daily Word*,
and shared Haitian wisdom in proverbs.

Stones in the water don't know the pain
of stones in the sun.

He threw stones.
I have a scar on my knee
and more in the caverns of my heart.

Who will give a new heart and put a new spirit within?
Who will remove a heart of stone and give a heart of flesh?

He threw stones,
but we could once have
huddled together against the darkness,
carving our visions, painting our cave
of dismembered dreams.

    —*El Tepozteco, Jan. 2017*

If poetry is an invitation to live our questions, then how can we honor our silence amidst so much noise, and dare to live our questions with fierce imagination and centered generosity?

If poetry is a window, a gift that must keep moving, a solace and sanctuary, then how can we broken vessels bear water for those in shadow and fear?

If the way of love leads always, how can we follow the call?

Katharyn Howd Machan

Bright Speck

When she opens her mouth
an egg appears
as if she's Leda upside down,
as if she's a chicken
in a fairy tale barnyard
where every door is gold.

Her mother and father were
both magicians—hats full
of rabbits, a sword through
the gut—and she grew up
with glistening mirrors
angled to tell silver truth.

How does she ever talk
to our world? What lover
can kiss those lips? Remember:
her own birth was illusion
and she learned from the shining get-go
how to write poems with her hips.

Katharyn Howd Machan

French Coffee

he brewed it thick and dark
in that two-chair rented kitchen
where a single rose
in a cracked clay pot
bloomed pink
outside the twice-locked door

January in Marseilles
keeps blue shutters firmly closed
and steady stench
of bitter cigarettes
can find
nowhere to escape

I thought he'd be the same
sane man
I'd met and kissed as August sun
ripened hard red blackberries
I thought I would be safe
with him

beer and beer and beer
through midnight
rage and hate and grief
tightening his trembling hands
stained brown
with years of nicotine

he tore to shreds
my notebook poems
he slapped me hard
for being nothing
worthless woman
in his anguished eyes

I pretended I agreed
I kept my passport safely hid
and when he went

to buy more smokes
I forced the window free
and fled

Poetry has been my core since 1967. I have shaped my life around it as my pulse and bloodbeat. I write for others to respond with their senses, their own curves of mind and body, stories old and new, breath of why we go on. I work to reach the deep and shape it wide: love and death and laughter. Light within dark, an articulation with rhythm: startling rainbows, colors people need in their sky.

Siham Karami

Elvira

She swallowed pain kept in her core of blue
and recognized my sinking shore of blue.

She wouldn't tell me where she came from,
an island where there's always more of blue.

The only nurse who wore an old-school cap,
she raised her son by night shifts, each hands-on chore of blue.

When waves of insult drowned me and I wept,
she washed my shame out in the pouring blue

And warned me of the agony ahead,
how men must burn us, make a whore of blue.

When his crazy rage erased my voice, her eyes held on,
a buoy in the room's uproar of blue.

She stopped me in the corridor, my heart closed shut;
I couldn't speak—deep in a war of blue.

Siham, she said, her eyes all red with mercy.
I wish I'd said, *Elvira dear!* But lost her to the evermore of blue.

Siham Karami

Interconnected

Watching us stand steadfast trees,
veiled and deepening in the indiscriminate light
of dusk imposing its hour
taking, undermining, turning
as we seek a fleeting incandescence
yet want the draught of nothingness.
How we argue in the parking lot, at odds,
throwing our thoughts to the shadows
where nothing feels secure
anymore. Anyway,
a few lone columns survive the paving
haunted by the ghosts of underbrush-dwellers
who would now be asleep.

We too prepare for death each night.
I cover you with your forlorn sheet
gingerly, your injuries a verdict against
my hands, which must pull you
right and left, lives riveted to body functions,
our minds like wandering wildebeests—
a stray thought, young and boundless,
soon devoured by a pack of carnivores,
my poems mere arrangements of the carnage.

The helplessness coded in complaints—
stop pulling this! you hurt my back!—
and I, the silent rebel, hide
among the turkey vultures in the branches,
my mind a surreptitious cloud
whose answers mimic rain,
the hum of falling.

Siham Karami

Romancing the Muse

Is it entirely natural to call a ghazal "verse?"
Slow down. The whole train's going in reverse.

For you must conquer mountains, monsters, mangrove seas.
How many miles did ancient pens traverse?

Leave the dishes dirty, piled like leaves.
Ignore the bleating flocks and walk into the forest, verse by verse.

Your ocean? Language. Dawdle at its feet
and dip your ears into the roaring waves of universe.

So what if you are drowning in great horny dreams?
Verily, the hour's rush of bees ends in its inverse.

Everything you are exudes the honey. Let morning cells
ooze their marmalade as rhymes converse.

With floodgates open, let the muse begin
his birdwatching, calligraphy, and swarms, heady and diverse.

And should he jolt or lose me in his pounding tides,
inventing names and cover stories, Siham is not averse.

Poetry is my survival tactic, a means to access difficult and essential truths, and a way to create an otherwise unachieveable space for my self to stretch out into without interference and simply be. As a caretaker for a loved one, my time seems more imaginary than actual. Only through imagination and the re-creation of memory does time become real and practical for me. It gives the inexpressible room for significance, enriching life itself.

Carol Amato

Good-Hearted Woman

His name was Willie which probably
drew me to him that first time his rig
pulled up too close to closing and we
had just turned off every piece of
cooking chrome there was.

It wasn't me but Marge who said she'd
make him eggs what kind did he like
over easy he said in that raspy voice
that really got me going imagine at my
age.

Marge said he even looked like Nelson
with that reddish braid down his back
but I said nothing maybe nodded.

I served him his eggs at the counter
with white toast and left-over homemade
sausages I was going to take home and
black coffee he said with one lump in
one on the side in case it was strong.

Thanks, Deb, eyeing my badge a good grin
wrinkling corners of those blue eyes.
Ate quick, wiped the crumbs off the grin
and pocketed the napkin with 'Just Barb's'
and a picture of the place and info.

Hope I see you again leaving looking back
at me pink now.
I'm Willie. See ya'.
Honest to God, he was humming
Good-Hearted Woman.

Carol Amato

Nocturne II: Day's End

Soon the recurrent dream
at the end of the day
every day's end
wiping the bottoms of all
the salts and peppers
ketchups
hot sauces
sugar dispensers
and everything else
that can be lifted
stacking the menus behind
the carousels except for the
daily specials which I toss
scrubbing the formica tables
and counters
cold in winter elbows kept off
the same in summer hot arms on
turning the bleach cloth over
and over, rinse it, again
and again
wiping the chrome
sweeping
refilling
restocking
tipping out.

Next morning
Can I warm your coffee?
Can I warm your coffee?
Can I warm your coffee?

Carol Amato

Lily: Her Cancer

She's been here as long as me
a regular
sits alone in the only blue vinyl
sometimes seems lost in her
thoughts but smiles straight away
when I come by with the menu
she doesn't need but it's a habit.
No need either to say 'the usual?'

No matter how many tables wait
we chat about the news bad and good
the kids hers, mine who fade in
and out of our lives depending
never the weather she says:
Why?
You can see it out the door!

Her paisley shawl often drops
so I lift it back around her shoulders
with my usual squeeze of affection
the catch in my throat when I feel
her diminishing.

From early on, I don't remember being driven to write poetry! Somehow, it happened, and I had little control. Even as a child, words sought me out. They found me and still do, even in the most peculiar places: hesitating over an iridescent puddle; face-to-face with a dragonfly; feeling the electric crack of a baseball bat in my palms; the face of a lifer waitress who I somehow knew. She found me, like all the other words did, and so I offer some of her to you.

WENDY TAYLOR CARLISLE

MAKE IT UP

> *"Remember. Try to remember, or, failing that, invent."* —Emma Donoghue

Every day, water: the lagoon, its angelfish ~~and Sergeant Majors~~, the harbor where the plane landed, the sea that roistered against my thigh~~, the river that licked my ear~~. There was clear water and bath water and seawater and river water and the evening cocktail.

Let's have something to drink or something with fish in it.

Sprinkle and moisten and splash and slobber and drool and drench.

Let's run through the hose stream, the drizzle, the big hurricane.

~~None of the wet makes sense.~~

How to fathom boats in the street after the tremendous wind, your grandmother, rowing? How to comprehend trips to the marina and beach and dock and port and mooring, along a through line, the wake behind the boat of the past?

First, devise the girl. You would like her to be laughing and lobbing her curls but she is serious and stubborn. ~~It hurts~~ when the nun combs her sopping, tangled hair. Arms akimbo best describes her. Difficult they say. Make me, is her favorite phrase.

Outside tick-fat raindrops stick in the window screens.

But if you're making her up, couldn't you make her happy?

I don't know how.

Grow her up beside the Atlantic, on A1A where the ocean comes back with a gulf stream of small memories that wash over her calves and ankles and leave behind a scum of regret, her history, a ~~difficult,~~ succulent project that rolls in like a tide with little pictures of the past that leave a line of small bubbles and scum across the beach.

Take the gift~~, I say to myself~~. Take the gift of the sea beyond the Pillars of Hercules of the Humboldt Current and the Atlas, Atlantis, Oceanus. If you don't like it, make it up. Tell it before anyone else can. When you eat first you always get the best bits.

WENDY TAYLOR CARLISLE

ALL OF THEM

> *Before you write a poem, you have to create the poet to write it.* —Antonio Machado

How does it become a thousand stories?
One by one.

"OOOh, honey, this bra is killing me,"
its spirals of black lace made of moving circles.

A ribbon at one hip? Jazz hands? Can it dance?
Is its hair a cropped cap or dark ringlets?

It has a soft spot for a guitar in someone's hands,
for a man's hat so perfect in this loony bin.

Oh yes, it likes to play—
hip-hop or a gavotte astride a hard-backed chair.

Is it a battle rabbit in a slippery boy's body?
Does it embrace everything underwater,

everything in its sightline? Can it plunder
all the muddy clay of Giverny,

all the muted light, the snake tree,
the ribbon tree, all the fall foliage at

the river's edge? How many of secrets equal
how many outright lies? All of them.

WENDY TAYLOR CARLISLE

IN THE YEAR OF OUR LORD

Things happen one after another. During the winter, Matt gets stuck at a four-blast crossing. The oncoming train gathers speed then squanders it. His death is less weird now than when it was happening. In spring, a journalist is fired for fabricating interviews with Sharon Stone and Brad Pitt. He defends himself by calling it "conceptual art." Late summer reaches us with its afternoon heat, brutal as a mishandled pit bull, with Canada geese in an overhead flotilla. It comes on in a body blow of afternoon air, settles on our shoulders like a hundred houseflies. In time, fall rain stones the cow pond. Don't leave the house then without a sweater, a patriotic conversation. All year long, humans find courage in Moonshine, spies offer sex for information and town square buildings teeter on the edge of disrepair. All year long the unmasked leap, battalions of flags and sweat sweep past. All year long when I try to talk about suffering a caul is over words like bully and shove. By December, I want whatever caresses me for need or pleasure. Who doesn't love a dark harbor?

Poetry because my head fills up with words and I have to make poems or I will explode. Poetry becasue prose confuses me with its cargo, its burden of words. Poetry because poetry susurrates and moans and sighs and whispers and sings over my shoulder. Poetry because it is in every corner, around every dogleg turn, because it is dilemma and euphoria. Poetry because without poetry, what?

Nívea Castro

BRUJAS

You were late to work this morning
te detuve hasta las tantas
And, I still feel you.

we danced last night, all night
You there. Me here.
synchronized fantasy flight

my skin tingled when you first appeared
four fingers clustered across my face
alluding to fragranced embrace

thousand miles and misty streams
Brujas somos, a witch's brew
emerging immersed in delicious dreams.

A steamy song heard just that day
stuck on one line played on and on
AMAME…en aquel lugar amor

traced the curves and turns
of thirst on your skin
with the edge of my lips

kissed right there where
soft flesh eclipses
honeyed female scent

honeyed
female
scent   of you.

You, were late
for work this morning,
 again.

Nívea Castro

TANGO

You soft say my name once, twice
first-touch back massage
scrambles my resolve
kisses spark an eddied urge
 a tinge of timid
pero *tranquilo bobby tranquila*
Tango dancing. Bachata rhythms. Old school R&B.
story sharing, shared meals
we "forget" to brew the tea.

It's been a while.

Like riding a bicycle, I remember
your name on my tongue
follows your frame
to free-flowing perch,
moves smooth and steady
as deliberate a song by Smokey's Miracles.
oh my Goddess, oh my Goddess
say you again and again. Morena,
que lucky que somos Lesbianas.

NÍVEA CASTRO

TOLD

I'm a first born of a first born
of a first born I'm told
the first natural born
native of immigrant parents

an only daughter on my mother's side
one of 50 plus grandchildren
one of five or so Lesbians and a bunch of gay boys.
I was wanted, I'm told.

In first trimester, third month
my given name arose in a song
she sang while pressing foot to the peddle
of a sewing machine in a Nueva Yol sweat shop.

the Voice in her head commanded my name
means *pure*
means *wombin seer*
because "this baby is born to a mission" she heard.

I'm told I kicked, I turned and curled
in time to her sappy song sung off key
my mother obeyed her triplet
holy roller Voice in her head.

I was born early morning
sag rising, Capricorn sun and moon
eight months from the day my mother
married pure, wedded virgin so I'm told.

During my youth, poetry was about and by dead white men. When I returned to New York to see my brother through his passing I experienced my hometown with new eyes and came across a poetry workshop facilitated by a passionate poet. Her passion infected me with a thirst to write my truth through poems. As an elder, my 'retired' left-brain has partnered with creative and artistic experssions: Social justice through the love of poetry.

JP Howard

COMPLICATED PRAISE POEM FOR SUGAR HILL, HARLEM & HER SECRETS

grandma said "chile don't you know we don't air our dirty laundry,"
that summer i asked why mama tried to kill herself years before.
"your mama just fine now. anyhow, you sixteen
and know best than to ask those questions.
you was just a little girl back then, all you need to know is she alive.
don't **EVER** let me hear you mention it again, you hear me girl?"

we bury our secrets in plain view,
carry them in our bloodstream until they kill us.

this a praise poem for secrets that get out
the womb, the grave, the psych ward, the damn door
praise secrets reaching through cracks in cement towards light
praise secrets that leave a body before becoming septic.

i cradled my secrets like a stillborn child,
stone still against a beating heart.

i held onto family secrets like a precious stone for decades.
now i sprinkle my dirty laundry everywhere,
take ragged pieces of my past and
stitch a quilt of monarch butterflies.
watch them fly away.

JP Howard

LOVE IS A WOMAN

after Pat Parker

Love is a woman.
When I feel her skin soft
against mine,
I am home again.

Then,
I forget Grandma
screaming at 18-year old me,
"I can't believe
my damn grandbaby
is a bulldyke!"
I forget Grandma's prayers,
her pleas to God
to make me
stop my foolishness.

When I touch my woman's softness,
lips searching for home,
our skin ablaze,
then I don't hear Mama
crying over old love letters
she found from my first girlfriend.
Where had she gone wrong?

JP Howard

Two Tankas for Trayvon's Mom

Trigger: black boys walk
off the street into my heart.
Before burial
her baby had that same spark,
same laugh, a place to call home.

Trigger: call Mama
baby, before the casket
becomes your new home.
Beautiful black boys beware
the walk home on a warm night.

"Why Poetry?" Poetry at this sexy, self-assured, and sometimes vulnerable 50+ stage in my life, allows me to explore topics that I once considered taboo. Poetry now allows me to unearth family secrets and to celebrate all the parts of my complicated self. There is a level of "I don't give any f**ks" that is part and parcel of embracing my over 50 self. It's been quite a journey to arrive here on the page.

Katherine DiBella Seluja

Wild Daisies

The summer my sister lay ill
we moved the painting of the wild daisies, hung it near her bed.
The bed was also moved, to the window, so that
after a morning of dozing, she could easily turn her head
and see the neighborhood children running tag,
hear the rumble of the mail truck as it approached,
watch the late afternoon arc slowly
across the wall.

Katherine DiBella Seluja

As she had planned

Weeks after *no further treatment*

she began
to say goodbye to the parade

of friends streaming.
To hug her daughters to fold

the wool sweater. To gift away
knitting needles, acupuncture set, carving knives.

The day after, a tattoo, a curling active letter
wrapped around a heart at her wrist.

Her doctor said it had to happen.
The nurse said *here's the little bottle for when*

She wanted crimson and cinnamon.
She wanted Celtic dance.

A celebration of passthebottle round the yard family
from Arkansas, Texas, Española.

She asked *how many drops below the tongue*

She dreamt of foxes climbing a gate in a field
the small brown bottle

of glass of sky of red velvet cake
and those magical candles that light and light and re-light

no matter how many times they are blown.

Katherine DiBella Seluja

Harvest

I found a single peach
growing at the center of the tree
the year the spring frost came late
and every pale blossom touched with a hint
of harvest turned overnight into crumpled newspaper.
And yet somehow, one blossom had survived.
Protected by a nest of branches that held the warmth
reflected from the trunk, enough to call the flower forth,
make good on the early promise sent from months before.
The fruit, larger than a bovine heart, much larger than my fist
surrounded a central branch so that one side faced west and one side east,
large enough to catch the filtered rays of light throughout the entire day
as the sun arched across the sky and pushed and urged this harvest forward.
This was the fruit I found on the tree planted for my sister, the one planted in her name.

As a young girl, I was cast as the studious one and my older sister was the artist. She painted. I read. I loved words. Precise words, heartfelt words, musical, lyrical, descriptive. Still, I wanted to paint. Early attempts at songwriting turned toward poetry and story. Now I see I am painting with words. When I capture a moment, a breath, a birth, a branch and set it into motion with language, I am full.

JOANNE ESSER

VIEW AT FIFTY-FIVE

after Jim Moore

1. The snow is part of it, gentle and inevitable,
   How it settles over every rough surface.
   And perhaps the last streaks of sun at dusk.
   What used to be rushed is calmer now.
   I breathe in the subtle colors
   Of sky, water, winter-bare trees,
   Perceive their infinite shades of difference,
   Something I failed to see
   When I was younger
   And so much in a hurry
   To accomplish all the items on my scrawled lists.
   I pour a glass of red wine,
   Answer your question about how my writing is going
   With a small smile, a sigh
   And look out the window again.

2. How it settles over every rough surface.
   I breathe in the subtle colors,
   Something I failed to see
   On my scrawled lists.
   I pour a glass of red wine
   With a small smile, a sigh
   And look out the window again.

3. Perhaps the last streaks of sun at dusk,
   Infinite shades of difference,
   Answer your question
   With a small sigh.

4. Something I failed to see
   When I was so much in a hurry,
   How it is going—

5. I look out the window again.

Joanne Esser

Summer Accounting

You count up everything you've been given
and what you can't have.
The sum is contentment and longing,
pushing and pulling at each other.
To the longing, you say:
There's a sliver of light at 8 p.m. that touches
the lifeguard chair across the silver beach,
shining the last mosquitoes and flickering
on dunegrass that waves in a darkening breeze.
A dead carp floats in the weeds, eyeless head
looking up toward the first star.

To the contentment, you say nothing.
June at the edges of things, turning
to July as you walk and walk.

I have been writing poetry ever since I was a teenager—through early love and loss, mothering and middle-aging—because it is the best way to discover what I think and feel. In poetry's conciseness and the pressure of its lines, words can be distilled to their essences. When the words come out right, I feel elevated, as if I can touch the edge of an idea that hovers just out of reach.

Judith Sornberger

On Letting Myself Go Gray

Not the dull façade
of a granite tombstone,
but the sparkle of moonlight
on the church bell.
Not the bell's bleak tones
at twilight, but the silver
music of a stream
curling through thick woods.

No longer the girl of gold
tresses swinging her basket
of scripted mercy,
not yet the wizened granny
trapped under shivering blankets,
I crawl into she-wolf skin,
her deep nap a wild shimmer,
as she escapes the cage of story.

Snout twitching, she steers
by her own scent, scrambles
upward to the ridge and stands
in the open, silhouetted
by stars, howling joy
into the endangered moment.

Judith Sornberger

This Autumn Morning Arrays Itself

in layers of sheer mist before
the almost naked mountain
like a bride in a distant century
preparing to wed the man
she did not choose, yet wrapping
her shy skin in one layer
of silk over another,
slowly—a bird folding
in her wings after flight.
Finally adding her finest kimono—
dove gray stained
with crimson maple leaves—
and tying herself
with an obi of the same
burning apricot as the oak
wears outside my window.

Autumn is always an elegy—
even this one, after living
thirty years with the man
I choose again each morning,
waking in his arms folded
around me like a gown
that knows my body perfectly,
embracing and forgiving
every imperfection.
Then comes the moment
when I step, alone,
into the chill of late October,
the dress rehearsal for
what comes next.

Judith Sornberger

Just this Once, Just this Much

a Zen saying

The homeless shelter asked if I'd drive you to register your kids for school. I offered to buy us breakfast biscuits at Dunkin Donuts first. Your teenage son helped the little ones with drinks and straws. Once we'd finished eating, you asked if I would take a look at your staples. You'd had back surgery just days before. Someone needed to check for signs of infection. *I could have done that, Ma*, your son said. You ignored him. I'm sorry. I don't remember his name or yours. *Watch the kids*, you told him as we left the table. The tiny bathroom stank of human waste, and the sink was dirty. You straddled the toilet backward and pulled up the back of your sweatshirt. Like a giant zipper, the staples climbed your back from waist nearly to neck. How simply some wounds are mended. No redness, no swelling. We were done. I wanted to hold you. I wanted to run.

By this point in my life, after many decades of writing poetry, it has become the natural way for me to celebrate all the quotidian joys of life, to grapple with loss, to reach out to others, to express gratitude for my existence, and to make sense of all the beautiful craziness of human relationships. Reading and writing poems continues to offer me a way to deepen and grow and become better at cherishing our world.

P.V. Beck

Rivers

Rivers are arteries of color running through a wild land.
Dusk turns Fox's river into a flame
a turbulence of dream songs rushing into darkness
where rivers flow into the sea
and seas empty into a sky filled with a bright scape of stars
leaping in arcs of picaresque constellations.
All night long Fox stalks shadows above the river's mercurial gleam.
As day breaks she flees her arterial world
through the hues of sunrise—
paintings on rock gardens, frescos on gray cliffs.
Polished soft Fox is the color of agates.
Rivers rake an untamed heart beating in rhythm to its shifting song
like the shining moon caught in whirling foam
like a shimmering fox running home.

P.V. Beck

The Seam of Time

Frost teases its way over the meadow each colder morning
the leaves turn
and pines stiffen in the waning afternoon sun.
Insects tumble in uncertain hatches over the pond
bees drugged heavy with pollen bury themselves in fading flowers
caterpillars crawl with a purpose
spiders freight their webs with moths—
things that crawl seep into crevices
and things that fly vanish into a failing light.
Dusk by dusk the ring and rasp of crickets drops away.
One morning the edge of the pond is frozen,
a congregation of red-wings conkarees into the chill air and disappears.
An hourglass tilts at the edge of the tipping earth
where Fox picks her way along the creek
cracking the eggshell ice along its watery seam.
She is part of a mystery at work in the slowing current,
the brittle hours,
the jigsaw pieces of a world congealing into winter.

P.V. Beck

Out of Place

Fox has no words for hand grenade or explosion,
she has not seen fruit split open, trees in splinters
or bomb blasted craters gouge a shaking earth.
Fox knows the words for whirlwind and thunder
she has seen ravens' shadows
tumbling through branches ahead of fire.
Fox senses our ant-like humanity from afar,
twitching an ear as the fiery day turns into evening
as the sounds of war trickle away into a hot summer night.
In a place out of place
she feels the weight of ripe pomegranates in humid orchards
hears the rhythmic rote of waves on distant sands.
Fox walks up and down upon a stippled earth
and back and forth upon its frescoed skein,
while overhead, scribing their fortunes on dancing thermals,
ravens glide home on a canyon wind
the molten twilight on their feathered breasts.

I write poetry to remember. The roar of pillaging and lying drowns out silence and wonder. The creatures most affected by climate change and the violence which it spawns have no voice. The Gray Fox is one of those creatures. The worlds she inhabits are the places language comes from and where metaphors are born and take flight. The Gray Fox's wanderings through the days and nights are a sketch of our own possible journeys.

Susan Hodgin

October Mourning

> *The life of the dead is placed in the memory of the living.*
> —Marcus Tulius Cicero, 106–43 B.C.

On this country road,
you might be on the lookout
for mule deer or whitetail,
but this Monday morning,
you slam the brake pedal,
close your eyes, cry
*I hit it! Oh, my God,
I hit it!*

Your heart hears
that thud, thud, thud against glass,
sees feathers
flying, sees blackness,
eyes close, darkness.

Your heart pounds,
no longer silent within you.
You stop the engine—
tears flow
as you roll the crow
onto gravel, settling it
below frosted, white yarrow,
towering mullein.

Before sundown,
you return—to find it gone,
not there anywhere!

Looking up,
you think *coyote.*
That makes sense—and go.

You trudge homeward
from the barren road
through perfect paths,

and stop to marvel at the strangest sight:

Behind the red-stained barn,
in the empty horse paddock,

a murder of crows perch, one-after-the-other,
bird-by-bird, unspeaking, side-by-side,
all black,
the length of the grayed-out fence,
all facing the lost crow
you left in mourning.

Now it lies raised—
wingless and fallen—
among over-grazed grasses, over-run ground,
lauded
before nightfall and evening star
by its own darkened flock.

Susan Hodgin

Sub, Assigned Drawing, Third Period

As students filtered into the room, a girl
glared at me approaching, stopping,
not knowing my name, not introducing herself.

She held up
her right hand, fingers flexed,
explained how she hyper-extended her fingers
catching a soft ball without a glove. "I see,"
I said—and watched her take a seat on the floor
beside a boy. He, already sketching, sprawled
across an unfinished stringing of a tennis racquet.

I found a Blick board, sketch paper, two
drawing pencils. Returning
to the gawkish girl, "Try this," I said
and jabbed a pencil between my teeth.
The class chatter grew soft, then hushed;
they stared as I leaned closer to the paper, neck bending
crane-like to reach the hard surface, pencil-piecing
lines like black and white television screen static
from the 50s—showing the girl—she could draw.

I removed the pencil, told the class
a painter's story—a woman, who had been shot,
left paralyzed without the use of her hands. Before
they could interrupt, I spoke to the girl, "You can—
use your other hand, if that's easier."

Poetry began as a classroom exercise, the writing teacher writing. Then, I found myself reflecting about what I saw in the natural world, a refreshing contrast to my desks—at school and home. My poetry is often prompted by an observation, a curiosity, finding a voice to tell a story. And that story haunts me, although its subject is not a complete narrative. But it must be spoken, filling the air.

Eileen Toomey

Drag Race

We watched RuPaul when my daughter was anorexic.
Her therapist sniffed, but we had fun with the show
because there is nothing better than drag queen drama
when you're fifteen and you have a mental illness.

Irreverent, fun and serious, tragic at times,
turning female stereotypes on their stiletto heels.
Ru says, *If you can't love yourself, how the hell
you going to love somebody else? Can I hear an Amen?*

And on opposite ends of our couch, we swing our arms
and snap our fingers, me and Claire.
RuPaul understands what it's like to suffer for a body
you invent, and the queens:

Sharon Needles
Raja
Alaska
Bianca DelRio, Peppermint, Adore Delano,
Shea Coulee

they twisting all those expectations,
changing silhouettes with padding and makeup and duct tape.
Is there much anorexia? I wonder, but I can't say that to my daughter
and I can't say *I am your mother and I love you. I would walk over coals....*

Charisma
Uniqueness
Nerve
and Talent.

Don't fuck it up,
Ru warns me

and I bite my tongue.

Eileen Toomey

He Sleeps In My Room

after Sharon Olds, "Nullipara"

We sit on the couch in our striped pajamas.
My father sews a button back on my mother's blouse.
He doesn't have anything better to do as he is dying
in my mother's house—the home she made
after he left. *I look at you,* he says. *All you kids,
and I think maybe I didn't do everything wrong.*
I make a face like bacon and eggs because I am sixteen.
Big jars of cancer drugs the color of taint are stacked
next to the bottle of strawberry Ensure,
the lampshade is tilted so he can see the four tiny
button holes with half moon glasses. *I do love him,*
I think as he snaps the thread like he's not sick.
Dad, I love you, I say awkwardly. *Yep* he yawns.
We watch *The Price Is Right,* cronies on the couch.
He is good at guessing the Showcase Showdown.
You would think I was the one who did all the shopping!
he says. But my mom did everything. I won't carry
him like a mother, he'll be a shadow instead.

Eileen Toomey

Dirty Water

People around here smirk at the sight
of an above ground swimming pool.
But in Chicago back in the day
we had a four foot high striped one
like a tin drum with an aluminum ladder.
When the water turned muddy,
my dad cemented the whole backyard
so we wouldn't track in dirt or grass.
Goddamn thing is filthy, he said,
cigarette hanging from his mouth,
mirrored aviator shades, hair slicked back
and ruddy red skin from tinfoil sun baths.
He banged the skimmer like a machete
on the side of the pool, knocking off
grass, sticks and flies.

Half the yard was cement anyway
for boys, for basketball, for skating.
At first it was fun having the pool
in the cement backyard. Then kids
grew up and tired of swimming.
Days went by, nobody went in.
Teenagers from across the alley
threw trash over our fence into the pool.
Empty cans of Old Style, a Kotex,
half of a candy bar, even a dead fish.

When I was eleven my dad left
our family and I was a chain link fence,
sinking in the four foot waters of our pool.
Nobody wanted to vacuum it,
the water turned green, so we took it down
and had big hole in the cement yard,
a dirt circle the size of our old pool.

The next year it filled with weeds.
We stopped going in the backyard
and weeds grew and grew. Sometimes

my mom paid me and my brother
ten dollars each to pull them
but the work was hard, the sun was hot,
and we were city kids with soft hands in the 1970's.
So the weeds developed thick stalks
like baby trees. From the back porch
it looked like a rain forest on a plate.
I'd think about the rats and alley cats
who lived there and shudder.

I hated our backyard
with the rusted basketball hoop,
without a single tree or blade of grass
only chain link fence, cement, weeds
and my heart wrapped in wool.

I am Sinead ripping up the picture of the Pope. I can't help myself.

Kimberly A. Collins

Hand me Down Mean

> *Aggravatin' Papa, don't you try to
> two-time me/ just treat me pretty, be
> sweet!/ I gotta darn fourty-four that
> don't repeat.* —Bessie Smith, "Aggravatin' Papa"

Probably ain't nuthin worse than a hand me down mean.
A mean you can't even say is wholly yours. A tattered
torn at the seam mean; a you don't know who owned mean.

A feed my belly mean to keep from crushin me.
It was my momma's and my momma's momma's mean.
A mean to fight. A mean to whip 'em good if NO was no good.

A two sizes too big mean. A mean I had grown up in before
I had a chance to wean. My daddy's mean. My man's mean
dat got no safe place to go 'cept up in me. A stay alive mean.

"Bessie mean" folks say. They only know a secondhand mean.
My Blues is mean. Folk like Bessie's blues. The truth is mean.
You gotta be mean to tell the truth and drink the truth most days.

I wish I knew who this overcooked, leftover mean belong to?
I wish I knew how much mean I had up in me.
I wish I knew how to bring 'em out one by one.

Kimberly A. Collins

Bessie's Men

Their Want hisses, straightens naps cradling my neck.
I tingle. Lips moisten. Desire is not shy. It flits, flitters, flutters
flies above the Stroll's moonlit streets. Primitive rhythms fling
It into frenzy. They say, they love me to make me stay.
Giggles tickle my throat at their believed trickery.
They do not know. I live free. Love's glow is not what makes
me shine or rise my wings. Boys are more trouble than men. Men
know. Money makes me nobody's—but mine. Wife, Mistress, Queen,
names do not alter the course of what's living in me. Love's weight
does not ground my flight.

I have known men.

Kimberly A. Collins

Paris Blues

His grey frayed scarf limply languishes
drunk with cologne,

Paris lights dim. I sniff its wool strands;
his scent lingers.

Unwashed musk, masks time;
it's a threadbare thing.

whiffs of him remain

What my truth looks like now as a woman over 50 is different than that of the bold 20 year old poet who had not learned to temper her language to get something said. My poetry now is an amalgamation of the selves I have birthed, imagined and claimed. It is my mission to look under layers of text and life in search of the real texture of intangible things to go beyond disciplined spaces.

Kate Hovey

To Bluebeard

I wipe layers of filth
from your laptop keyboard
recalling the lock you bought
at the Pont des Art bridge
the cold oiled heft of it
fingering our names
scraped in the metal with
that knife you kept so handy
how you wrapped a chain around
the lamp post and kissed me
your breath heavy as you
clicked the lock in place
tossed the key into the Seine
our arms linked watching it fall
like a golden fish glinting
the moment the sun struck
before darkness swallowed it.

Think of it buried for decades
crusted in layers of filth
love-tokened sediment
so much now locked away
your Darknet links double
password protected
hiding a tale too old
and we both know what lies
on the door's other side
raw things split open
empty as the glinting fish
I've watched you gut
your breath heavy
blood runneling the sink
the cold heft of the knife you
still keep handy scraping
scales off to strip them
of their golden flash all
that fleeting beauty.

Kate Hovey

Lilith Utters Ineffable Names

> *...and he said, 'I will not lie beneath you, but only on top...' Lilith responded, 'We are equal to each other inasmuch as we were both created from the earth.' But they would not listen to one another. When Lilith saw this, she pronounced the Ineffable Name(s) and flew away into the air.* —From *The Alphabet of Ben Sira*, 800-1000 A.D.

That's right, lover boy, all seventy-two—remember?
Maybe I skipped EHEIA (what the eye seeth not)

nearly choked on that one *for now my eye sees thee*
went straight to JOD instead (Ruler of Adam) oh, baby

talk about the tail wagging the dog, your real ruler
betraying you, still standing at sad attention—stiff

with hope—as I breathed AVOH (I will come) oh yes I did
while your face brewed a perfect storm *I will satisfy my fury*

so I shouted ESCH (the name of God which soundeth fire)
then NA (to be uttered in perturbation) and more, but who's counting?

Snake-eyed, spouting your venom, clenched jaws came unhinged
when I slipped into claw and wing—so easy, then—my cloak of feathers,

screeched BIGDOH (God's garment) and HU (God the Abyss)
what a hoot—the Big Zero. Staring into that blank face,

pitying the poor saps to come, I cried HEY (breath of God)
five times, a panted measure, and YADOH (God's hand)

shooting up like a plume of hot steam over the forked river,
the crush of heavy air thick fingers clutching my throat.

For years I've asked: why has the word 'feminist' become so onerous—the new F word? The death of iconic SEXUAL POLITICS author Kate Millett coupled with the White House reign of an unabashed misogynist (who famously called his opponent a "nasty woman") makes exploring this quesiton even more pressing for me, as a poet. As an ancient history/mythology buff, my search for any answer inevitably leads me in one direction—back to the beginning.

Pamela Gibbs Hirschler

The Chibok Girls, One Year Later

Those other girls
rescued in May, stand atom belly to back
in a rippled line,

we deploy troops to search for kidnapped girls

218 of those 234 other girls are pregnant,
after capture, rape, forced labor,
rescue

we run for Congress and condemn the kidnapping of schoolgirls

none of these 218 were the Chibok girls
who, it is said, are gone—

we investigate a Chibok business man for complicity

what is the half life
of our interest—or action—to
bring them back?

we organize a candlelight vigil to mark the anniversary

John Donne said no man
is an island. 2,000 girls,
kidnapped, sold by Boko Haram—

we hold a panel discussion on the Chibok girls problem

my country
sends cell phones,
special news coverage, 80

80
80
80 troops—

and our congresswoman urges daily tweets so the world will not forget

The Chibok girls are an island.
One year later—tell my government
they have oil wells

in their vaginas.

Pamela Gibbs Hirschler

To Build a Universe

I.

Begin with nothing. Survey your surroundings. Add the hiss and click of the infusion pump. Rest your right arm straight on a pillow, prevent the high-decibel occlusion alarm. Push the call button when you need to go to the bathroom. Wait until the aide comes to unplug the pump so you can roll it with you. Don't wait too late to push the call button. Or, don't push the call button. Unplug the pump. Roll it to the bathroom door. Don't wonder if it will tip over. Loosen the bolt with your left hand and lower the pole of the pump stand so it fits under the bathroom doorframe. Pee in a plastic measuring bowl. Wipe with your left hand. Wash your hands for 30 seconds. Dry your hands. Rub your hands with sanitizer gel. Use a paper towel to grab the pole, roll the pump back to your bed. Plug it into the wall. Toss the paper towel in the trash. Smooth out your sheets. Get back in bed. Push the call button. Tell the clerk the plastic bowl is full.

II.

Watch the TV news. Someone will die. It will be a bomb, or a knife attack, or terrorists with guns in a place of worship or a wedding or a funeral, or someone with a gun will shoot a policeman, or a policeman will shoot someone without a gun. Any of these killers and victims may be of any race, nationality, religion, age, or gender. Turn the TV off to stop the drone of voices in your head.

III.

Salivate each time carts roll down the hall outside your closed door. When your door opens, remember to thank the dietician for bringing your food. Sit on the side of your bed while keeping your right arm perfectly straight. Don't sit on your IV line. Remove the insulated cover from your dinner plate. Lay it upside down on the foot of your bed so the condensation pools in the lid. Don't wonder if the fish is wild-caught. Eat one bite of beets with your left hand. Eat an entire soft whole grain roll with your left hand. Forego butter—it requires two hands to pull the lid off the packet. Eat all your mashed potatoes. Eat all your peaches. Pull plastic wrap from a bowl of chocolate pudding. Don't wonder if it's sugar free. Reuse the plastic wrap to cover the beets.

IV.

Watch the TV news. There will be a political convention. Many people will give speeches. Some will protest. All who protest will be escorted out of the building. Some will endorse a candidate. Some will not. Some will wear strange hats. Turn the TV off to stop the drone of voices in your head.

V.

Fall asleep. Wake in 15 minutes when the aide rolls in a cart, take your blood pressure and rolls a thermometer across your forehead. Ask what your numbers are before she leaves the room. Fall asleep. Wake in 15 minutes when a lab tech brings another cart. Close your eyes when they insert the needle into your left arm. Open your eyes to watch your blood pour into the specimen tube. Feel the snap as she pulls the rubber tourniquet off your arm.

VI.

Watch the TV news which will not report that Native Americans are protesting a pipeline that will cross their sacred lands. Scan through all the news channels without finding the Native American protests. Try to understand the absence of reporting. Turn the TV off to stop the absence.

VII.

Thank the nurse for offering to show you how to turn on the TV. Tell her you prefer the quiet. Listen to the doctor explain your test results. Ask appropriate questions. Try not to ask him to repeat himself. Ask if you will go home tomorrow. Ask if the biopsy will hurt. Thank everyone who comes to your room. Take a shower with a plastic bag taped around your IV tubing. Be surprised at how grateful you are to be clean. Watch the helicopter fly past your window as it lands. Feel guilty that you are grateful it's not coming for you. Imagine your health is the same as it was five years ago. Meditate. Pray. Do yoga stretches in your hospital bed. Start walking for 15 minutes back and forth in your room every hour. Tell the doctor you feel better. Wonder if the pipeline construction has stopped. Leave the TV off so that you don't know that somebody else has died. Leave the TV off. Leave the TV off. Leave the TV off. Leave the TV off.

Pamela Gibbs Hirschler

Evangelical Admonition to a Young Girl

Don't

look
stare
speak
argue
think
undress
menstruate
wear a bikini
read seditious poetry.

Poetry has become my way of bearing witness and of finding what has been lost. Poems are explorations. Poems are discoveries. Poems are memory. Poems are reactions. Poems are connections. I use poetry as excavation into what it means to be human, woman, lover, mother, daughter, sister, and to weave all of these threads into some sense of myself and the world around me.

MARIEL MASQUE

GENESIS

And I thought,
let there be folds.

And there were dark-pink,
velvet soft, labia creases.

And I said,
let there be water.

And a river rushed from her base,
washing her rich terrain.

And I said, let there be a breadth
between her waters.

And the tip of my tongue
traveled the length of her hips

and I made her expanse open and stretch
for seven nights and seven days

And her pleasure I named heaven
and her moans warm summer rain.

Mariel Masque

Self Portrait

Hot chili pepper body,
curvy torso,
plumb breasts,
bird of paradise head,
peacock-fancy hair dress,
and fish tail served over crisp lettuce bed.

A tempting sea nymph,
I dance on stone plate.
Roasted pimento scents the air.
Like in flies,
these compound eyes
watch multiple realities at once.

Go ahead,
try to eat this *sabe-lo-todo*
who grew up next to the asbestos plant,
breathing fine glass,
sweating pesticides,
head sprayed with DDT for the lice.

Mariel Masque

Birth of a Poet

When I was 9, longing to reach my adored abuelo,
I tried to swim back to the island from Palma Sola Beach.

I got sucked by the riptide.
There was no lifeguard on duty.

With all my strength,
I swam to reach the surface.

My legs cramped.
As the asthma attack evolved,

the pull of the undertow dragged me to the depths.
I watched the last bubble of air float toward the sun.

Hours later, I woke eyes sculpted on sand
and coughed streams of salt.

Hair entangled with Caribbean seagrasses,
My scratched tongue wetted the cracks on my lips.

I rose from driftwood,
diatoms and beach wrack.

Wearing the cloak of a starlit night,
I walked home sobbing.

"Where have you been all day, muchachita?"
Mami screamed.

"Fishing."

As a former refugee and a queer Caribbean mestiza over 60 with a congenital disability, when I write poetry, I embody the Babylonian Goddess Ishtar and perform the Dance of the Seven Veils, stripping until I stand naked. My poems destroy the shackles of the construct and reclaim my true essence. Poetry is my homeland; the sacred space between chaos and order where my issues, cultures, languages, roots, and worldview matter.

Lynn Valente

I was a pencil

I was a pencil for Halloween.
First I grew my head to a point
of weighty darkness
yet persisted in holding up
the wooden mask protruding
from the top of my gown.
My gown was gold and orange
painted onto flesh
and embossed
with my number,
nationality
and the finest 2-word poem I'd ever heard:

> Venus
> Velvet

In the moonless night
I ate my candy on the run
from house to house

Since I had no baggage
unlike my sisters,
the witch and the princess.

Lynn Valente

Flute Player

Spotlight on her fingers and their tiny gestures

Invisible targets for her breath
mounted round the room

Tilted princess   wooden door   bamboo shadow

Audience drowning in polite water

Mouthpiece warm against her chin

Audience cuts loose from gravity   floats up
toward the ceiling

Her breath now

must hold them there

Lynn Valente

Literary Love

I tried to make you love me
by mouthing some words from a book

I didn't know
you'd picked up my book, let it
fall open to just that page
on which she is trying to get him to love her

Those words happened to become
available to me
as in learning a foreign
language: to get them
to pass you salt at the table,
say *these words*. But now
you think I'm a literary
person, a literary love

And I am ashamed
as if you had undressed me
and found my clothes
paper
my heart
ink
my skin
more paper
with nothing of interest
to read there
my whole body
a pencil
trying to write you down

Poetry is a conduit for what's true.

Sue Churchill

I think of the Greeks

i. Return of Spring

A season diseased, missing its morels, trout lilies, trillium--snuffed out
by the invading species, fruitless pear, bush honeysuckle, that outstrips
the saplings, portends the wood's degeneration. I pull the garlic mustard
in the yard, the barn lot, along the road until I come upon squads stretching
off into the field and forest, hundreds, thousands, hundreds of thousands of white
wands sprinkling seed to hatch below, the heads mostly empty. I am stopped
in despair, left like Psyche at her labors, but no god to bring small armies of relief,
reinforcement.

ii. Cock of the Walk

The rooster thrice attacked, left three wounds, deep and round. He'd been picture-
pretty— Rhode Island Red, feathered in that royal blend of deep green, rust,
and scarlet. A shining comb and princely demeanor, the rooster in cartoon. And all
was well for him until he made himself my husband's rival, came for him, again,
again, lay in wait. So small in all he hadn't seen, could not foresee: the ax, the gun,
the hand never laid against him in all its unseen power. Even caged for execution,
this fool strutted and squawked: *Just wait—what I'll do to yooouuuu!!* What delusion, what
hubris. He would be dealt with at Their pleasure, when They got around to it, left hung
by offending spurs to drain in the flock's full view.

iii. Neither Grey-Eyed nor White-Shouldered, but Dark-Hearted

I, too, play my part. I watch the menopausal Silver Wyandotte attack
the young Ameraucana of the pale green eggs, bring her beak like an awl to spill
blood around the filled feeder, keep to herself what I have provided. And, though I
know to let them mind their affairs, I intervene like Athena, swoop down, shoo
her away, see my prized hen eat in peace.   But when I step away, they choose again
their chaos. Their cruel pecking order, useless in this place of protection and plenty,
will once again prevail.

Sue Churchill

Executive Order, January 2017

I found the bodies of dead doves
left to rot in the grass, their soft spotted grey,
rose underbelly soiled, the dropped necks, dented eyes—
the ones who amiably peck for leftovers
under the feeder and in the beds, who don't
confront, who rock along as if incapable of haste
but flutter if they must, to cover.

The doves, who know their own heaviness,
like the pregnant girl, her swollen body
beyond her own control, the mother, heavy before
or after child, who cannot keep up
on the road, or the old, old lady,
who cannot carry her own load.

The doves, the easy prey for dogs
who never before took notice
but now, the young one has discovered
this sport and spoil, the doves
one by one, brought down, done in,
and to no purpose under heaven.

Because sometimes I'm full to bursting, because it helps me out of ruts of thought and opens up fresh pockets in my mind, because there are things I can't make out in the haze, except through the prism each poem holds up, and because the moments tumble on so fast, only poems seem to hold them in place. Because, in the end, it is the only language of love.

Ruth Mota

Billie's Brazilian Ghost

We hear your plaintive call,
echoes of *Yemanja*, goddess of the sea
succor to women in child-birth
to grandmothers cutting cane
to young girls whose bellies rise
before their breasts have blossomed.

Your rhythm pulses in strong brown legs
a heel grazing a cheekbone,
quick crouch and a cartwheel
capoeira death moves masked as dance
dreaming of a ruptured jugular.

Your harmony limber as the foot of a thief
who steps over shards of glass
rising from a stucco wall,
lithe as barefoot boys on the beach
who transform soccer balls to acrobats and comets.

Your craving as fierce as the woman
who upends our garbage cans on Tuesdays
scavenging for remains of last week's dinners,
as passionate as the thousands who fill the teeming streets
of Rio and Sao Paulo clamoring for justice.

Strange fruit hangs low in our hearts
while fire lilies unfurl from your throat
blooming in a voice laden with ashes,
champagne bubbles rising in a smoke-filled room
chains creaking in a service elevator for a diva descending.

Click of handcuffs on your deathbed
heard by ghosts in holds of galleons.
Oh Billie, raise your voice just one more time.
Let the filled concert halls see those poplars
where we pray strange fruit will never hang again.

Ruth Mota

Brazilian Honeymoon

Into the maze of Recife's canals the couple meanders
lit by a sunset soaked in the sweetness of tropical wonders:
graviolas, sapotis, carambolas, jabuticabas and *cajus.*
fruits with names that curl like cats' tongues over matted fur,
bursting with pungent flavors exotic as their names conjure.

A mellow green sea gurgles and laps at the shore
where the woman stops to sing of desert folklore,
of the moon silvering solitude, of guitar and heart strings ringing,
where her voice rouses from rocks below a host of rats
whose beady eyes stare fixed and frozen by her singing.

She moves on with her beloved, into the banking district
where sultry women curve their serpentine spines against marble doors.
His fingers stiffen and sweat trickles through her pores
when a voice of sand and mangoes murmurs to him: *Want to make a baby, honey-cat?*
when a man staring at her whispers in his fat friend's ear: *Wish I could afford one like that.*

They find shelter in a restaurant where they dine
on coconut-covered fish and sparkling wine.
The waiter, dressed in black, stands guard, one hand behind his back.
For dessert he brings a white rose and a note with fruit and cheese.
We are honored by your genteel presence, it reads in Portuguese.

Such a torrid, tumultuous affair in the bowels of this place
whose burning breath comes tumbling with them in their honeymoon embrace,
where strange night sounds turn out not to be
enchanted rats in rafters summoned by her song,
but bell-boys scurrying for a better view of their fervent ride till dawn.

Ruth Mota

Pechisso's Tale

You hunker down. Home at last,
your ursine body unwinds from our day's journey,
your enormous black hands wrap the arms of your chair,
hands that just yesterday sewed up a man's leg severed by a crocodile,
hands that today steered me safely through Mozambique for the first time,
through the flooded valley, around landmines and past bandits
who flashed headlights ordering us to stop.

We rest now, relieved to have arrived under a night sky raging with stars,
under a doorway riddled with bullet-holes. I ask who shot here and
you unleash the story of Portuguese rule, of local men, forced from their land,
under threat of bull-whips lined up right here,
men protesting injustice, shot in front of others, right here.
You tell of the fight for independence, of the truce and treaty and retreating Salazar
        army,
of one soldier, irate at a boy wearing a T-shirt proclaiming *Viva Frelimo!*
and of the shot that broke the treaty, killed the boy, whose death triggered the massacre,
wild wielding of machetes and the call to kill all whites, right here.

And you, Pechisso? What was it like for you?
Silence echoes between us. A chorus of frogs croaks in the moonlight
and you sigh like the sea before you spill your tale.
Accused of conspiracy for protesting torture
of a man whose bloody wrists you treated twice,
you're thrown in prison without warning, without trial, without charges.

Trapped in a cell not wide enough to lie down,
nor lit enough to tell dark from dawn,
a straw mat to rest on, a hole to pee in,
only cabbage and *chima* paste to eat until your body shrank to flesh on bone.
Two years in total darkness, seven hundred twelve days,
until you're released into the blinding light.
The bus you took home robbed, you knelt on the road
under a blazing, unfamiliar sun, and railed: *Oh what an unlucky man I am!*

Only at home, your wife nursing you to health,
did you find the pain too much bear and nearly killed yourself.
And to me now you say as you stare into the star-riddled sky

as you sit under this door raging with bullet holes,
to me alone you confide, or perhaps to no one in particular,
Sometimes I still think I am lost.

Poetry is a healing art, a path to self-discovery and social change. I write to re-examine life in bite-sized chunks, to grasp our shared humanness, and find social meaning by facilitating poetry circles with prisoners and veterans. Poetry allows all of us to dive into beauty, to observe more clearly, take ourselves less seriously, shape our hopes and dreams into rhythmic prayers.

LYNNE McENIRY

POEM

you driving north.　　me
home with weekend chores, yet if
we close our eyes and
listen to the calm between
our phone lines, we can see the

Pollack there on the
museum wall before us
hear the docent ask
us to consider how the
painter can quicken a line

by thinning it, brush
tip barely dipped in black or
how he can slow it
down by flooding canvas with
blues dripping plump from the brush.

Lynne McEniry

If I were to die

I'd want you to know
I dreamed of cooking
my mother's beef stew for you
your freckled legs swaying
from the arm of your chair

I was at the counter
trimming fat from the meat
leaving just enough
for a deep brown gravy

You were reading to me from *the city in which*
    I love you
choosing my favorites
guessing at others we'd soon hear
the poet read

the space between us
filled with the scent of sweet carrots and
a common language

    This Room and Everything in It
    Lie still now
    while I prepare for my future,

I peeked under the corner
of the bright blue tea towel
to see how the bread was rising
you read

    certain hard days ahead,
    when I'll need

stopped before the line
break, or no—the alarm clock made
its demands so I rose and wrote
down my dream.

Lynne McEniry

Summer Afternoon on Aquinnah Cliffs

I drink in fresh sea air today
each pore in my body opens
itself, inhales centuries of wisdom
from the ancient salt that blankets me.
I lie for hours
in the green grass of Aquinnah Cliffs.
Below walls of clay that protect
Moshup Beach, reflect aquamarine,
where a pod of humpbacks swim
filtering fishes through baleen, releasing back
gallons of water.
They feed blowhole to blowhole.
Every night they breath consciously from beneath
                 only half their brain sleeps.
Up here there are spirits
to guide me.
Whales and Wampanoag
whisper to me their legends.
They are never written down.

Why poetry? mystery, community, crew, beauty... craft, curiosity, creativity... honesty... good and true poetry is free of borders and boundaries and censors... a space where many experiences and ideas and ways of knowing, ways of expression can be explored... there are spaces for utter silence and mad noise... poetry embraces everyone who comes to the table... poetry knows suffering and hate and pain and loss... and it knows hope and resilience and peace and beauty...

Lynne Santy Tanner

On this Bright Day

Yesterday, searching for my work shoes
in Elizabeth's far barn,
I discovered a tumble of mice under a blanket.

They looked at me with such terror
I closed the wardrobe and left them
but today, Marcus and I are going after them
with a bucket… *Once they're in it,
they can't crawl out,* he says.

We open the armoire,
pull away the blanket.
Two scurry. Three, with coaxing
actually go into the bucket to be released
back into the wild…

Reluctantly, Marcus sets traps
baited with peanut butter.
Our task here complete,
we head back to the work of painting and sculpting

but on the path, a fawn
so small I could pick her up,
her eyes, wild like those of the mice.

Go find those we set free, I say.
Tell them not to come back.

She bursts into the air
all feathered tail and spots
and with two gambols is in the tall grass.
She looks over her shoulder once then is gone

and the mockingbird I've heard all morning
lands on a branch over my head.

Silhouetted against the sky,
I see her beak open and close,
her pitch perfect for this bright day.

LYNNE SANTY TANNER

MIDSUMMER

The days of June
seem longer than ever I remember,
the sky so late
fading from pink to pearl,
still aglow after ten o'clock.

I am a child again going to bed by day,
up at dawn.
The clear morning air
carries me all the way to blazing afternoon.

In my garden
orange daylilies dance
arm and arm with purple iris large as salad plates
and bee balm buzzes beside bold rudbeckia.

Along the highways sumac flames.
The sun,
blinding me as I eat,
turns our dining room gold.

Now by decree
it may go no farther,
but must retrace its steps
across four mountain tops
as I begin to count the days.

I cannot stop this up-speeding
towards autumn, but I remind myself,
still to come, the lovely light of August.

Lynne Santy Tanner

The Mocking Bird

Before leaving to visit Suzanne, I walk my road
as though I'll be gone years instead of days.

The Hawk is scolding loud above David's land.
David has been cutting pines all week
but the Hawk is angry only with the Crow.

Higher up the road I hear the Mocking Bird,
a good sign, then a "Georgia Bird"
      as my brother Chris
called the Blue Jays when we were young
      and visiting our Grandmother.

The Cardinal is silent this morning
though not hidden
as he weaves his red thread through the scrub
between Mark's house and the house of that new Neighbor

who is always working in his yard,
so serious, so diligent,

with so little poetry,
never stopping to listen.

And if the song goes on much longer
I will be late getting on my way
and have no time to write this down.

I write poetry to give voice to the things that overwhelm me daily: the inexplicable joys of an ordinary life, but also the unspeakable grief we experience.

Akua Lezli Hope

Algeria

I.

My lost friend, I loved the way her kohl-rimmed eyes
folded in the corner, deep like mine, how she shined
and burned, laughed larger than her small mouth
loomed larger than her petite body, trembled with strength
the languages that crowded her mind, French, Arabic, English
from Tizi Ozou, Berber of the Kabylie, freefolk, fierce
In Paris when I told the cab driver about her, he said
'They all claim that' like black folks once claimed
they were from Harlem but that is where I learned
to jump rope, slice ham and bologna in mama's store,
drew the arch filled with numbered squares
for jumping jacks, so I did not doubt that prison
she grew up in, that the French tortured her brother
that she met the Cleavers and no, not the ones of Beaver
though you may not remember either the banal panto of
repressed American domestic perfection nor the dynamic duo
she of coppice crowned 'do and he black leather jacketed
revolutionary, the romance of exalted struggle
distilled. My friend helped them in another
Algeria. I thought she meant night gowns
when she said pied-noirs

II.

She told me the Bedouins of her youth 50 years ago
had nowhere to go penned in cities they weren't born to
unable to ramble roam cross the sea of sand they once sailed
decameled and without milk or tents
the worth of their infinite world made finite,
their sky made small and their children swept like sand
through the city to find whatever they might find, to learn
lessons their culture could not comprehend
and she gave her little friend a milles feuilles, a thousand leafed tart
and her Bedouin friend summoned the children of sand
and shared, peeling each thin leaf apart

Akua Lezli Hope

Resurrections

They are a happy couple, comfortable
in their knowledge of each other,
relaxed bodies, smiles, conversation
a gentle teasing of the detective
who still doesn't guess his wife's motives
or his daughter's, but knows their hearts
better than any others and worries over all
between cases, strives to be good
for which they tease him when he fails

Makes me cry, as any good fiction
resurrects you, even the ones you wouldn't like
but would watch with mommy and tell me
you sussed it out before the end, saw it
coming even as you sat still for our rough
ministrations as we braided your balding ring
examined your thick nails, pinched, poked
and tickled.   you made her endless
cups of tea that got cold, you confessed
that you weren't superman. i cast you in that role
anyway.   what returns is the love
when the stone rolls away
what flutters forth is love
why they wept was not just for his tortures
but the loss of his presence, the scent of his sweat
his striving and kindness, his generosity, his huge heart,
blood warmth of his strong, large hand holding theirs
for the love they were left to carry
forth in the world, alone

Poetry is intrinsic to me. My first poems were love poems, dictated to my mother as I created poems before I could write. That anecdote reveals how I came to be. It was always and ever with words and through the encouragement and nurture of those who gave me words and supported my own tool use. Poetry is how I manage my concerns, explore, and bear witness. Poetry helps me see, manifest, and speak.

Julie Rochlin

Picking Peaches In The Dark

We can't see ripeness—
telling patch of rouge,
those low-hanging branches
needing rescue.
I root blindly until the furry orb,
more prickly than the soft we think of,
is cupped in my palm,
still attached to the tree.
Finally I get it. *The fur. It's armor!* A coat
for one too tender.
And without twisting
or yanking, just holding—
to say… *I'm here, if you're ready to go,*
my fingers await the drop.
It's the same light touch I used
as new bike-rider peddled off,
my hand behind the seat,
never knowing I'd let go.
And it's the same touch now
as I hand them fruit: peaches
they'll take to their own homes,
my hand cupping night's cool air.

Julie Rochlin

Recuperation

From the canoe
of our couch
his twenty-one years float

Suspended

My son's body
having made a lethal
time-bomb

The surgeon's cut

stitched and bandaged
our only proof of what we hope
he banished

Time is shaped

by the sweep of plates
brought and taken away as once
I swept hair from his unsure eyes

Bolster to boyhood confidence

Inside this wooden frame
our home, our son's home—
though he's soon to claim another

we feel such false comfort

The old blue throw
wrapped about his shoulders
can't protect from what

we cannot see

The cells that rocked our safe
world. The word as alarming

as undertow—Still the walls console us

We follow instructions—

Help him be still
allow for mending
wait for news the harm's contained

Let us hold this

as between time
Let the day move on
without us

Julie Rochlin

Camp Ontario, 1973

Our heads almost touching as two loons
against an almost-night sky,
we collapse on a metal cot, damp suits
clinging to new curves, giddy from a mix of
lake-water and new-friendship, we exchange stories

Erica tells of her family's inn,
snowy Vermont walks to school—
You should come, we'd have a blast.
—Sounds great! I say, and launch into
New York City grime, hearing about this canoe trip.

We shiver. Tonight, the rustle of a canvas cabin,
but tomorrow, the wilderness…

God, I exclaim, *that swim test!*
I can't believe we're the first back.
Erica gasps—
You swore! My parents say it's a sin
to take the Lord's name in vain!
I ask—*Are you religious?* My mind
sounding an alarm like the ram's horn
I once heard in a synagogue.
Sure, we go to church and stuff.
Don't you?
Church…no, I'm Jewish - not religious.
Erica's eyes widen, then squint—
You…Jewish? I've never met one before—
I'd never know you're Jewish, no one would.
If you visit, don't tell my parents.

We sit on the edge of the cot,
spines coiled, feet seeking sure ground.
My voice comes out soft and measured.
What do you think Jews look like?
Oh. I dunno, Erica pauses,
twisting one bright strand of hair into a nervous curl—
Dark eyes…hooked nose.….something like that.

The screen door wails—
girls flood the cabin to change for dinner
and like Moses parted the waters, I see my escape.
I rise to join the others, not able to look back.
I don't want to know if the red sea closes behind me.

When I began writing poems in my 40s, it was to hold on to the all-too-fleeting family life I'd built. But as I've watched our government and some of our citizens go haywire, I find I have an apocalyptic reaction to name what I value, what the next generation might never see and what I'm afraid we all may lose.

Joanne Godley

Picnic

Keys to the kingdom granted
(My parents' bookshelves)
At age nine
"Read anything" (they said)
My chosen text: WE CHARGE GENOCIDE
A horror picture book; in black and white
Bristles the hair on my fearful arms
Turning page after curious page of
Gentile outdoor gatherings
Here a table set with treats galore
Shirt-waist'd ladies in their finery
Gents comporting smiles and cigars
Guileless children playing as children do
Their inheritances assured
While treed men swing with hung heads
Mouths stuffed full of coveted appendages
Sunlight shines through neck laced trees
Gracing a Sunday southern picnic

Joanne Godley

Bois Caiman Ceremony

Boukman and Cecile dance as rain beckons
Along black pig hide, an offering to
Seal the deal. Never captivate Haitians.

We gather, comparing mendacities
Wrought by those with the keys to the chains, while
Hougan and Mambo dance under the rain

In those infamous Gator Woods, the storm
Sparks souls to battle. Prayers rage on and
A blood-let cry: Never enslave Haitians

Staccato drums temper a high pig squeal
When clouds clear, the pig's head's meshed on a stick
The high priest and priestess orbit again

History alone will decide which dance
Was revolutionary, meanwhile, woe
To those who dare shackle a Haitian

The first in liberation in the west
Now, among nations, the poorest. Visions
Of Boukman and Cecile dancing magic
So all will know: Never chain Haitians.

Joanne Godley

Anatomy of a Scar

I have refrained from touching this wound; refrained I say
taped my hands at night; worn mittens; allowed the wounds to crust and scab over, then,
created internal distractions to stay far the hell away from myself.
when my son was a phd student at uchicago he organized a protest group
U chicago having closed their Trauma Unit forcing many South Siders
to bleed to death en route to an ER across town
the group leafleted, held talks, picketed, engaged and enraged the University for years
someone sent me a YouTube video of my son's arrest at one protest
Chi town cops surrounded him; he asked that they call the University 'cuz the protest
was sanctioned; those pigs took my 77-inch baby down; face down
then, opened ranks; the camera showing him on his face; on the ground handcuffed
My heart flash froze; I tried to squeeze my body into the YouTube
I wanted to shove aside those cops; slip off his manacles and say, "get up, Baby. Mama's here."
this drama plays on repeat in my head a zillion times each day each night
Trayvon Martin / Eric Garner / Sean Bell / Michael Brown / Alton Sterling et al
make the news for walking or running or speaking out or saying nothing or breathing or
simply being Black and human
silent tears well and crest inside
my pain is a wrapped box no one wants to open
the anti-gift; I am all black mothers to all Black sons
birthing them growing them launching them into the world to fight social wrongs or die
trying their exit wounds wound me linger deep crust over
taut tough scars I point but do not touch
this scar, that scar
"there, those be my sons"

Poetry fulfills me, drives me, comforts me—no matter the emotional state or the situation. I usually find or write a poem that defines it. Poetry was my first art form and continues to nourish my creative writing. As a daughter of the Diaspora I appreciate poems that speak to social justice issues past and present.

Virginia Bell

The Skin Essay
[excerpt]

Layer 1

In the waiting room,
one woman with an eye-patch,
white tape, white gauze.

Another with no ear.
What's left of a nose.
Men, too—old, young.

I put my earbuds in.
Begin to listen:
Skin cancer begins when

cells in the skin grow
uncontrollably.
To learn more

about how cancers
start and spread, see
What is Cancer?

How tautological.
How taut my skin was.
Now, a surgeon's sutures.

Squeamish—I mean *squa-*
mous cells are flat cells
in the outer part

of the epidermis
that are constantly shed
as new ones form.

Look! Your epidermis is showing!
my brother used to tease.
And I turned red, looked up,

down, for some unladylike
tug of cloth, skipped button,
sudden stain.

Layer 2

In the examination room,
it's cold.
Bright as ice.

The doctor tries to distract.
Or impress.
Dismisses *Anna Karenina*,

Madame Bovary,
(the anesthetic needle
dives into my face)

The Yellow Wallpaper,
even *Hamlet*
(the scalpel melon-

balls my brow)
as un-illuminating
tales of female madness

and suicide. Instead,
she recommends,
Eat, Pray, Love.

She has a crush
on Javier Bardem.
This is indeed distracting.

Layer 3

Back in the waiting room,
the seats are full.
A classroom at school.

A secret club.

A select sect.
Flash from the future.

Our punishment for looking
too long, for flying
too close. No,

for darning the sky
with our own excretions. One poke
too many and the hot egg's

shell exposed.
Supernova raw. Not like
the wooden darning egg

that used to nest in my mother's
mending basket, alongside
remnants, tins of buttons.

It seemed so harmless,
sanded smooth
to the touch.

But no one lives
like this anymore,
repairing their own—

Layer 4

Back on the white-papered cot.
What is there to say?
It's a *Groundhog Day*

kind of pain,
the tug of the tool
familiar, thread's pull.

The surprise of being cut into
never gets old,
never dulls.

Layer 5

*Basal cells
constantly divide to replace
the squamous cells*

*that wear off the skin's surface.
As basal cells move up
in the epidermis,*

they get flatter.
Unless they're afflicted
with carcinoma.

Then they grow so fat and round they burst
from their little elevators
like pale, pink suns.

Touch me, they say.
Notice me.
I'm new!

But only your fingers
pay attention,
straying to the nascent nibs

while you read,
while you talk,
while you sleep.

Layer 6

Punishment? Too catholic.
This is not about sin.
This is about folly.

I wanted to be a cat.
To roam the hillsides
rubbing on the rocks,

traipse the meadows
on padded paws,

nothing but fur

on my back.
Now trapped.
Now sutures spit

from my face
like stubborn
white whiskers—

I only leave the house
in make up,
in human disguise—

Layer 7

No, folly is forgetting
about C.
I mean my friend

whose name begins with C.
Forgetting what lies
beneath *her* skin.

I'm not talking about melanoma,
the skin's dark basement
erupting in tiny earthquakes.

I'm talking about farther down.
In the hidden infrastructure
of her body,

the vast network
of bone, tunnel, and tissue.
The wild roots

overtaking. Like the time
the plumber dug up
my front yard.

The back-hoe's claws
raking right through

the main drain.

Oh C. forgive me
for dragging you into this.
Please C., don't go—

Why poetry? Because poems are adjectives for the world, for life, for death, for consciousness, and for the unconscious. Because poems are what Anne Carson calls "latches of being": they attach everything in the world to its place in particularity. Because I was a latch-key kid—and poetry is a means of attachment. I write, I read, I speak, I listen. I hold on.

WENDY MARIE VERGOZ

HIS FIRST WIFE

>   *and victory filled up*
>   *the little rented boat…*—Elizabeth Bishop

He caught her
like a fish.
That's how
he told it
when asked
how they met.
"I had to
get it right
just once," he'd say.
"I got it
right with
my first wife."
As he spoke
he would
demonstrate
precisely
how he'd played
the catch:

Right hand flung
behind right shoulder
left hand
in front of his face
as he tipped back
and cast
the make-believe line
which had
perfectly
snagged her.

Next, right hand
drew quick
small circles and
both hands glided
toward his jaw

as he reeled her in
deliberately.

She listened
to his story
and wondered
(as they were
still married)
at his use of
the phrase
first wife
though he said it
always
with a chuckle.

One day
his words
formed a hook
in her mouth.
She tasted blood.

So she
cut the line
and lived.

Wendy Marie Vergoz

Popsicle

It's a Popsicle,
he said
think that it's a Popsicle.
I said,
"I don't like it."
But he said
What about what I like?
Popsicle.
Lazy August evening.
Michigan.
Five years old.
Not this.

Popsicle, he said.
I said, "No."
And he said
Just for a bit
knowing
that I hated it.

Popsicle.
Julie and me
on banana-seat bikes
zipping home
through fireflies
for Popsicles.
Not this.
Not this Popsicle.

When I read
of the Sofitel
housekeeper
in New York,
I think about
Popsicle, think that
I think about

the screened-in-porch

in Michigan,
five years old
I hold a melting
Popsicle
think that it's a
fireflies blinking
in August's hot air
Popsicle.
Think that.
Just for a bit.

My manuscript, The Unbinding, *chronicles the experience of a woman who survives domestic violence and sexual abuse. I believe it is imperative that women survivors use their voices to bear witness, especially given our current political situation in which sexual assault and abuse of power reach to the highest levels. More personally, Why poetry? Because writing poetry helped keep me alive during twenty-seven years of domestic violence, and it now helps me to recover.*

Bo Niles

Why I believe in ghosts

I open the door to your closet
and sniff wondering how long
the stringent whiff of your skin-scent
and your green plaid flannel shirt
will linger even as I know
someone has already rummaged
through the used clothing bin
and now wears the shape of you

Bo Niles

Topography

Bereft of a cartographer's compass
I must rely on the graze of fingertips
with their papillary ridges to decipher
the braille of chanced impressions
across what once had been my breast.
(Fingers fit so neatly in the Y-shaped gulch
formed by the fine white tines of scar.)

But for touch, orientation isn't so easy anymore.
Benchmarks blur; contours erode; and bas relief
is void of relevance. Now all mapping devices
(that compass, for instance) skid across skin
that once defined that slope I truly believed
would ground me for life—before being
bared to the happenstance of what it hid.

Poetry became the passion of my life when I retired. Subjects have evolved as my life has transitioned, from work and family, to creating a new self after losing my parents and husband and surviving breast cancer. Friends and family (and poetry buddies) offer support now that I (not only I) confront how all I/we had hoped for in this lifetime (clean air/water, healthcare, etc.) is under attack.

Arfah Daud

Younger Days, Growing Up

We eat what our aunt cooks.

Mother shops for dry goods
once a month; a 50lb bag of rice,
tea, coffee, sugar, flour, Milo,
sweetened condensed milk,
soy sauce, catsup, oil, oatmeal,
flour and a big tin of crackers.

When Mother brings home
dry goods, we get excited.
It's a celebration for us.
A symphony plays
endlessly in my head.

We help put things away
in containers, happy
to see food fill to the brim
Canned goods arrange by size.

Mother tells aunty
Make it last the month.
Aunty has to ration, to control
the kitchen tightly. My brothers,
always hungry from school
would sneak into the kitchen and
steal crackers.

Mother shops at the wet market
for vegetables and seafood
on days the fishermen bring in
their fresh catch. She goes
and bargains for her goods.
Aunty waits for Mother to drag
home her bargains before she cooks.

Sometimes we wait until 3
to eat lunch. Aunty cooks

one time a day. It is always rice
with *Assam Pedas*, or *Curry*, or
Masak Kicap, and veggies.
She portions for lunch and dinner.

She hates it when I invite
friends over for lunch.
She'll have to cook for dinner.
Mother will get furious,
scolds her for making extra.
I pretend not to understand.

At a young age I only care
that we have food to eat.
I can invite friends over
to taste food from our kitchen.

Arfah Daud

Will I Survive the Kitchen Sink
10 years old

Aunty gets uptight with me.
She complains that a girl
like me can't do anything.

*Why study hard. You'll
end up in the kitchen anyway
when you get married.*

*Learn to sew, to cook.
Learn to sweep the floor
clean the kitchen.*

At my age some girls are betrothed.
They'd be taught the basics
of keeping a house.

Aunty nags too much.
She gets tired of doing everything.
She needs an assistant.

I am still playing tag
with my brothers. Sometimes,
I borrow my brother's friend's
racing bike and ride around
the neighborhood.

Tired of her nagging,
I said I will help.
I will only wash the dishes.
I will not sweep the floor.

My bratty brothers dump
everything in the sink.
After lunch it's a war zone.

Heaps of crockeries pile
high haphazardly.

It takes forever to wash them.

With this much work to do
I'd rather not get married.
It takes too much effort for one meal.
For a whole day's worth of work,
will I survive?

Arfah Daud

Hooked

Every day after school
I eat what my aunt cooks.
Today we have rice
egg *sambal*
and young jackfruit
in coconut milk.

My aunt also fried
some salted fish
for me.
She knows
I'd enjoy it.
She is grateful
I have been
doing the dishes.

I eye the sink
and see disaster.
I hate my brothers.
The twins especially,
they just eat and run.

I pinch the salted fish
and my aunt says
I should try wiping
the table after the dishes
are done, then
sweep
the floor.
That way
I'd get one part
of the
kitchen done.

Next time I'll teach you
how to cook.
I will also make you your favorite dish.
My taste buds stop dancing.

I want to scream,
but instead
I smile at her.

I enjoy reading poetry, especially, the ones that move me. I write to paint stories so my children and grandchildren would know about my childhood and about life in Malaysia where I was born, about growing up with many brothers and sisters.

Tricia Cosca

Rules of Engagement for Combat Robots

Take time for your relationship to grow.
Don't go galloping off to the minefield;
stop and consider one another's lenses.
You will see yourselves reflected.

Use I language.
Instead of, Put down your weapon
or I'll shoot, try, I need you to stop
pointing your weapon at me.
It makes me feel that I have to shoot you.

Stick to the behavior, not the robot.
Remember that she was programmed
to plant that IED, just as you were
taught to remove it.

Lean on your extended families.
Let your elders prepare soft beds
of lavender for your marriage, to grow
through your engagement.

Learn from them, but cultivate your own fields.
Watch their tiller's spiked wheels plow
through knotted grass roots, spitting
rocks and flowerpot shards that sting
limbs and tear eyes, like marriage fights.

This may remind them of doors slammed,
a hairbrush thrown across the room, but now
sweat rivulets like amniotic fluids run
down their clay-glazed, spider-veined calves,
watering the soil they loosen to allow

root spread and easy growth. They wish
just enough rain and sun, for you.
Lavender is hardy; the tiller is tough.
You will know better than they did, when not to shoot.

Tricia Coscia

Thakil

> *Appear weak when you are strong, and strong when you are weak.*
> —Sun Tzu, *The Art of War*

The father taking pictures knows that loss
decomposes. Like his child's skin gone to soil,

it regenerates, fuels his calves, he walks
and walks, flavors his eyes, he sees and shoots,

ignites his heart, it grinds on like the gears
in his photographs of orderly things.

It flakes from his son's painted tarps, the blacklined
figures that carry the weak among them

in fields where viruses multiply. He
replaces his son's wet brush and canvas

with a cold lens, resumes the contrast,
the harmonized patterns, restores the order

that fell like the green plum, before the yellow,
when the white haired one was left

to see off the black haired.

Tricia Cosca

Carrying to Term

1981

We drive in Rita's green Pinto to the clinic,
every six months, pee in plastic cuplets, try not
to smudge our names before we slide our samples
through the mini door—snap it shut to alert
the lilac robed tech who collects our drips
and releases them on paper strips
like tiny paint store swatches.
She watches for their colors
to change, while we scan
glossy Cosmo's

and make fun of Glamour out loud,
although covertly, we slip the weight loss tips
under our tongues. The waiting room is painted mauve.
Rita calls it pussy pink, wonders why the doctors can't get enough
of the shade. We laugh until our names are called; one of us cranks
the breast-exam view-master, hurriedly, so the demonstrator
hunts for lumps in fast-motion. The other is stripped,
redressed in paper thin as the sky, covering white lies
with small talk, pretending she is not splayed open,
her shame shielded from the world by nothing
but a vinyl curtain, blush-cheeked despite
having read *Our Bodies/Ourselves*
from our mothers' nightstands.

We leave with our treasure sacks
stuffed with six pink shells that open
to stiff viscera arranged like the clock,
little pills ticking inside. Buckle them in
our army surplus backpacks. It will be
another year or two before
we realize—even this
won't protect us.

2016

We knew what to expect
before we expected anything,
read *Whole Child/Whole Parent*, sealed
every outlet before we risked bringing anyone
into our uncertain world. For our daughters'
third and fourth birthdays, along with tutus
and matching magic glitter wands—
we gave them pretty princess words:
Aureola, Labia, Clitoris, unleashed
for them to sing with abandon
as they rode fierce and fast
on berry colored bikes
and always

wearing their helmets.
As their breasts came into bud,
we introduced them to our fears
disguised with royal names—Chlamydia
Gonorrhea and Papilloma; shielded them
with Gardasil and coin purses full of Trojans.
Today our daughters hang their ankles
with confidence in the metal stirrups
behind the curtain, barely wincing
as the midwife impregnates them
with the tiny pickaxe babies

they will carry for the duration
of the presidential term. They don't cry
when their Achilles scrape, as they pull their feet
from the cold steel stirrups. Each womb bears
a warrior daughter: Para, Mirena, Liletta,
and Sklya wait in the quivers
to sterilize lovers' quarrels
while the mothers
prepare.

Poetry addresses the spaces between, what can't be said, the indispensable, bare elements of our stories. Writing poems focuses me on the essential details of my lived experience and helps me remember, understand and process those experiences and the world surrounding me. It is a way of sharing understandings that ordinary conversation or writing cannot articulate.

Margie Shaheed

LifeCycles

1

Moon-colored candles cast black shadows on yonder walls of women
dancing fiercely. Bantu hips sway and gyrate to syncopated rhythms
of fluorescent lights and icy chrome. The path outside the canal
leads to village cultures which have faded into each other.
A mosaic of orderly chaos. Sun-dried hair lies well on the head
anointed with expectations.

2

The heart of the woman is filled
with children and bullet holes
like the Rwandan woman's belly is filled
with everything
       except food
            except blood
                 except embryonic fluids
and the Valentine baby is stillborn.

3

The moon eclipsed when she passed
wearin' nothin' 'cept molasses and a gold ankle chain.
Sand beneath her feet made wings
as bronzed hands guided here through
the light of prism darkness—mesmerized—
where at last she felt no pain.
Blue swirls rained from the skies,
showered her body/cleansed her soul.
Thunderous drums rumbled to the melodic
sensation of seven bells;
a chant was heard:

> *blue body I've known before*
> *the waves of your back sustain me*
>   *let me ride once more*
> *let me stand upon the strength of your shoulders*
> *blue body I've known before*
>   *let me lay my destinies upon your shores.*

                    4
Reptilian feet read like palms
lifelines deadened by the reality
of concrete and no shoes
trample across the planet of my mind
        scraping its surface with rough scales
        forcing me to abandon the sun to witness
        instead a morning dose of rancid air
        filled with memories of last night's fare;
        foil and plastic are disturbed
        by a rummaging pair of hands.

                    5
Dried blood smeared on concrete
pounds its sounds for deaf mutes.
Al wrote a letter from a Brooklyn jail,
featured his plea on primetime TV for revolution

And all the while talkin' heads scream
their needs into the atmosphere:
coffee, bagel, subway token, please.
        And Gil said, "The revolution will not
        [The revolution cannot] be televised."

                    6
Menarche rites not filled by concrete and smog
cause fertile Earth to burst,
to burst through indurate bedrock in exchange
for a warm place to circulate life's forces.
        And I heard the Ashanti woman say,
        "I alone can present the blood."

Margie Shaheed

WHEN WE GET TOGETHER

we give it up to the drummer

    between silences

        stroke the mighty bass with our toes
our nipples
    crashing
        cymbals

ting-ting-ting-ting-tinging

    head board a sweeping piano

we strum the hell out of guitars with elbows composed of love songs

    lips double dipped honey blows the flute

our band plays regularly in the middle of the night

        we don't care who hears the music

Margie Shaheed

Nostalgic Hair Affair

for Eula & Alicia

Your life, a shrine I've erected in my mind…
where today I see you sitting on the porch of our Hough
Avenue apartment in a ragged turquoise dining room chair.
Cotton sticks to the back of your housedress whenever you rise.
Barefoot, your toes wiggle against the warm concrete floor in cool
satisfaction of a large jelly jar filled with ice cubes and Pepsi-Cola.
The heat of summer and cornbread and pinto beans cooking
have long pushed you out of the kitchen.

Your life, a shrine I've erected in my mind…
where I hear you call me in from the dirt yard.
Poised for my next shot, I look up at my friend
because now we must abruptly end our game of marbles.
Armed with a brutish Afro comb and hairbrush,
you sit me down between your legs;
your familiar scent settles me.
As you grease my scalp with Dixie Peach
I can't help but remember the first time I met my friend Silk
> *"Do you know why dey call me Silk? Cuz, Ah'm sooo Black.*
> *If you was to rub some Vaseline on mah skin right now, I'd*
> *look jus' like a pair of black silk stockin's."*

Ouch!
I recoil from the pain of teeth
dragging through my resistant napps.
Smack!
You hit my hand
with the back of the comb
and tell me to be still.

Your life, a shrine I've erected in my mind…
where I feel you momentarily break away from your task
to sing along with a static-version of the Temptations
song blaring from our hi-fi.
Although I dare not turn around to look at you
I know your head is bobbing up and down

like an apple in water to the beat.
When the last lyric fades into radio announcements,
your knees tighten around my shoulders.
I wipe the beads of water from my neck,
the sweat that has dripped from the jelly jar,
and I fearfully brace myself for round two.

Your life, a shrine I've erected in my mind…
where my hair eventually loses the fight
        to six plaits intersected by crooked parts.

Life drives my poetic expression. I have always been a sensitive, observant person. Writing poetry allows me to voice what I can't always say in the real world.

Gina Valdés

Under the Eagle Sun

    1
In Northern Mexico
tías yelled warnings
to play in the shade
as we ran out of the house
to skip, prance, and spin all day
under the eagle sun.

    2
In Southern Mexico
dark men call out, *güera*,
as if saying, *querida*.

The eagle sun plants kisses,
darkens our faces.

Under a gold moon
tugging at the blood,
he whispers, *morenita*,
she sighs, *prieto,
mi amor.*

Gina Valdés

A Brush Dipped in Night Ink

Shizuko—mother-
in-law, was once
a girl with a brush
dipped in night ink,
composing haiku
on rice paper lit
by a paper lantern
and a watery moon.

Across a vast ocean
of sky, I draft poems
at dusk to the indigo
notes of a shakuhachi.

With inky brush
I stroke kana
on sheer paper that flies
to Shizuko,

between us a dusky world
lighting its lanterns.

Gina Valdés

Walking on Earth

On my walk on earth
may I greet everyone
with a silent blessing

walk steady on shaky land
soft footsteps on rocky soil
cruising crows soundless above me

on dark nights
walk with green birds
luminous jasmine

on full moons
walk with the flute player
a satchel of songs

walk on earth's edge
sky's rim
where worlds meet

On my walk on earth
may I greet all that lives
with a silent blessing

bless what must end

My life as a poet began at age five as I listened to my older sister read out loud the poetry of Sor Juana and other Mexican poets. I was spellbound by the concise, musical writing that could contain and express so much feeling: love, passion, praise, and resistance to what oppresses. And now, in the last stanza of my life, in tumultuous times, I feel an even greater urgency to write and publish poetry.

Joanna Rose

Apology to a Mother Long Dead

after Anne Sexton

I was that kind of kid
that stealing kind
dimes to quarters to shiny half dollars
that red leather purse where you hid
your coins your red lipstick your cigarettes and matches
your valium
that stealing valium kind
letting you think it was you—that kind
I was that lying kind
  Don't go into the woods, you said,
  I won't go into the woods, I said.
the bad boy woods, the wicked witch woods,
where I hid my stolen treasures
where I hid in hollow tree trunks
   covered with woodbine and creeper vine
and read fairy tales
   a good mother who died
   a youngest daughter who spoke
   and pearls dropped from her mouth
    precious jewels, gold coins,
    an oldest daughter who spoke
    poison, toads, snakes, lies
I was that kind, so happy in my lies,
and then how long it took to get to true
and the great curiosity of true
in dirt in sky touching everything I could
   hold break fuck love bury
hide in rotten tree trunks
me with the other eyes
my little sister's sweet white bed
all the the pretty castles I torched
with the gentlest burnings
I was that burning kind, that stirring kind,
   stirring the hot ashes still
   with your long bones

Joanna Rose

Death School

for Penelope

When death visits it leaves a door just barely open.
You think you can look through the crack, sniff
the air of that other place, but you can't, and you shouldn't.
Only being a good daughter makes you think otherwise.

You've been visiting with death,
flying back and forth across the country,
peering into your mother's old eyes to see if it's there yet.

There are death professionals like priests and physicians
and hospice workers, and even they don't look through the door,
don't listen for the calls of strange birds in that rare air.
Priests and physicians and hospice workers learn
in death school to open the door but not peek,
not eavesdrop on death's aimless and one-sided conversations.

You fly home, long flights over the whole wide country
and death rides along. Do you let death have the window seat
or the aisle seat? Does it fall asleep and drool on your shoulder,
onto that pretty brocade scarf you always travel with?
Do you read it the poems you write about it?
Does it snore gently in your ear,
does it talk in its sleep, do you listen
for it to say your name?

With the reading and writing of poetry my thinking seems scattered, but brightly focused, in small surprising ways, pieces of life in their particularity. I am bemused, or startled. I have come to understand this: I don't think in sentences but in flash of image, whole thoughts falling on my head and settling in pieces around my feet. It takes sustained effort to gather the pieces. This is an important way to live.

WENDY MITMAN CLARKE

COLD FRONT AT MIDNIGHT

Long across the bay
and folded fields
the wind tears me awake.
I flinch like prey

in the roar. Out there,
the waves are pleated white
beneath a needlepoint sky.
The seabirds share

a dark canvas, wing and gale
stitched in effortless seam.
I drift on memory uneasy
as silk, woven thin and pale,

unraveled by this change
in the weather, unsure if dawn
can mend this ragged night,
this tapestry so fierce and strange.

Wendy Mitman Clarke

Joe Pye Weed

All summer long the Joe Pye weed
stretched for the sky, growing madly
in the small garden by the door.

Truthfully, it wasn't the best place
to plant it, any prudent gardener
could have warned me, for if content

it would take over the whole bed,
shade out the timid, push past the weak,
block the view from the back porch

and, after a hard rain drape
across the grass, making mowing
problematic. All of which it accomplished

while endearing itself to butterflies
and bees seeking its tufted sweetness,
while speaking to stars, neighboring owls

and the murmuring twilight
as I slept by the open window hoping
for a conversation as enduring as this.

Even now in its dotage, brown and bowed
as an old man, its flowers furrowed
into stubborn brows of fuzz resisting

the pull of the wintering wind,
the nuthatches and wrens adore
its ragged cloak of leaves,

their sharp clutching toes reminding
the stems of their purpose. And though
it's just a weed that grows in ditches

and abandoned lonely places,
too tall and wild for my garden, why

wouldn't we dream to be Joe Pye weed,

to know the busyness of chickadees
scratching for seeds in the shelter of our bones
if that is all our bones had left to offer?

Why wouldn't we ache to climb and fall,
to know we are loved this deeply,
to be needed for so long?

My whole career has been made of words. Lots of them, all prose. One day about two years ago, I signed up for a poetry workshop, because I realized how tired I was of all those words. They couldn't say what I needed to say. The sear of writing poems gives me that freedom. It lets me be honest with myself and the world about pain, mistakes, anger, fear, emptiness, wonder.

Wendy Mitman Clarke

Note From the Tide, Falling

Broad Cove, Maine

Let me go now.
How else will I ebb true
and clear, all my edges exposed?

Let the terns pierce me
over and over. The eager dart
of their diving does not hurt.

Let me breathe out
to make up for the long breath
in, the holding of so much

water, the manes of weed,
the shoaling mackerel, the burden
of current and time, entangled.

I see you there, listening,
the sound of me slipping
through seaweed fingers,

your coffee cup chipped
and stranded on the granite.
You left it again in your distress

and bare feet, always needful
for some answer beyond
the logic of the moon.

Don't be so selfish, for once.
Let the rocks warm themselves.
Let me lip tenderly the broken shell

and cobbled ruin of the ledge
so the smallest animals see the sun.
Let the mud glisten like silver.

Let me change everything.

About the Poets

Carol Amato's poetry has appeared in several magazines and journals and she was nominated for a Pushcart Prize in 2017. She is also a natural science educator and wrote ten nature titles (Barron's Educational Series) and *Backyard Pets—Activities for Exploring Wildlife Close to Home* (John Wiley & Sons). She also provides nature programs for classrooms with focus on inquiry skills. However, in a previous life, she may have been a waitress!

Laura Apol teaches creative writing and literature at Michigan State University. For more than twenty years, she has led creative writing workshops in local, national and international contexts for writers of all skill levels. She is the author of several collections of her own poems: *Falling into Grace; Crossing the Ladder of Sun; Requiem, Rwanda; Celestial Bodies; With a Gift for Burning;* and *Nothing but the Blood*.

Pam Baggett's chapbook, *Wild Horses*, was a runner-up for the Cathy Smith Bowers Chapbook Contest and was published by Main Street Rag in spring 2018. Recent poems appear in *Atlanta Review, Cold Mountain Review, Kakalak, Nimrod,* and *Tar River Poetry*. Work also appears in *Forgetting Home: Poems About Alzheimers* and *The Southern Poetry Anthology Volume VII: North Carolina*. She teaches poetry workshops and hosts readings in and around Hillsborough, NC.

P. V. Beck's poetry, non-fiction, and fiction have been published under various names in books, magazines, and anthologies. Her focus has been on the figure of the fool and on patterns in the natural world. She lives in the mountains of northern New Mexico where she is also a musician, artist, and works on trout habitat restoration projects in her watershed.

Nan Becker's book of poems is *After Rain* (Elephant Tree House, 2011, elephanttreehouse.com). Poems are forthcoming or have appeared in *The Common Ground Review, Cloudbank 2, Journal of NJ Poets, The Meadow, Nimrod, New Millenium Writing, Redivider, Red Rock Review, Salamander, The Stillwater Review* and elsewhere. She lives in Stillwater, NJ.

Virginia Bell is the author of *From the Belly* (Sibling Rivalry Press 2012). Her poems and personal essays have also appeared in *Hypertext Review, Fifth Wednesday Journal, Rogue Agent, Gargoyle, Cider Press Review, Spoon River Poetry Review, Poet Lore,* and other journals and anthologies. She is a Senior Editor with *RHINO Poetry*, an adjunct professor at Loyola University Chicago and the Chicago High School for the Arts, and holds a Ph. D. in Comparative Literature. virginia-bell.com

Upon completing an MFA in Creative Writing from Hamline University (MN), **Brenda Bell Brown** will pursue a doctorate in media and practice. Her literary work has been published by Foliate Oak and BLACKBERRY: a magazine, several small presses and audio/visual recordings. She is most fond of the Saint Paul Almanac's publish of "Home is Knowing the Path to Her Door," a tribute to a dear, departed friend. Catch Brenda as host of the ever-eclectic "Play for Me" on KFAI Radio.

Wendy Taylor Carlisle lives and writes in the Arkansas Ozarks. She is the author of five chapbooks and two books. Her third book, *The Mercy of Traffic*, is due in 2019. Her work is widely available in print and on line, most recently in *pacificREVIEW, Artemis, barzakh* and others. For more information, check her website at wendytaylorcarlisle.com.

Nívea Castro is a writer and photographer. A three times VONA alum, Cave Canem workshop participant, and Hedgebrook alum, her poems and writings have been published in numerous journals and anthologies. In *Aster(ix) Journal*, her Cuba photographs were highlighted. She is also the curator and editor of a Lambda Literary Awards Finalist *Soy Lesbiana y Que! Out Latina Lesbians*. She has curated and/or been featured in various venues, mainly in New York City.

Sue Churchill lives on Thistle's End Farm in Woodford County, Kentucky, where she writes and raises sheep and chickens. Sue has degrees from the University of Kentucky, Northwestern University, and Auburn University. She taught for many years, beginning with teaching ESL for two years at Sriwijaya University in Sumatra, Indonesia. She taught longest at Woodford County High School, 1999-2009, and most recently at the Lexington-Fayette Urban/County Jail and Detention Center.

Wendy Mitman Clarke's poetry has been published or accepted in *Blackbird, Rattle, Little Patuxent Review, MUSE,* and *The Delmarva Review.* Her poem "The Kiss" was a Pushcart Prize nominee. Her nonfiction has been published in *River Teeth, Smithsonian,* and *National Parks.* Her novel *Still Water Bending* was published in October 2017. By day, she's director of media relations for Washington College in Chestertown, Maryland. You can read and view her work at wendymitmanclarke.com.

Kimberly A. Collins is the author of *Choose You! Wednesday Wisdom to Wake Your Soul* (Amazon Books), *Slightly off Center* (courtesy of a grant from the Georgia Council of Arts), and *Bessie's Resurrection* (Indolent Books, 2019). She received her MFA in Poetry from Spalding University and her MA in American and African American Literature from Howard University. She is a Callaloo Fellow whose writing appears in major anthologies and magazines. She teaches at Morgan State University.

Tricia Coscia, a recent MFA graduate of Bluegrass Writers Studio, writes with hope for social, racial & environmental justice. A runner-up for 2017 Bucks County Poet Laureate, her poems have appeared in *A & U: America's AIDS Magazine, Connecticut River Review, Parting Gifts,* and *Peregrine Journal.* Tricia thanks fellow poets, teachers, death-row exonerees and co-workers at Witness to Innocence, her husband, their children and menagerie.

Arfah Daud was born and raised in Malaysia. She received her MFA from Antioch University Los Angeles. Daud studied with Eloise Klein Healy, Richard Garcia and Chris Abani. Her poems have appeared in *Byzantium, Susan B and Me, The Mom Egg, Spillway, Sin Fronteras, SoloNovo, New Plains Review, Apple Valley Review, SageHill Press AWCH & Watershed.* Daud currently resides in Santa Cruz, California where she teaches high school.

Christine Ernst is a writer, poet, performer, teacher, activist, and frequent speaker, focusing on the connection of wellness, personal narrative, hope, and community. She works for an arts non-profit on Cape Cod and writes and performs a new one-woman show every summer as the *Fat Ass Cancer Bitch*. She believes that the story will save us all. For more information, visit her website, christineernstwriter.com.

Joanne Esser writes poetry and nonfiction in Minneapolis, Minnesota. She has also been a teacher of young children for over thirty years. She earned an MFA in Creative Writing from Hamline University and published a chapbook of poems, *I Have Always Wanted Lightning*, with Finishing Line Press in 2012. Her work appears in *Common Ground Review, Temenos, Welter, The Sow's Ear Poetry Review, Iconoclast* and *Ponder Review*, among other journals.

Joanne Godley is a physician, bioethicist, writer, and poet. She completed a certificate program in novel writing from Stanford University and has just completed her first novel. She has published narrative nonfiction essays and written a lyric memoir about working for the Peace Corps in Africa, excerpts of which are forthcoming in an anthology by the Women's National Book Association. She is a member of the Women's Fiction Writing Association and the Author's Guild.

Ruth Goring (ruthgoringbooks.com) has two poetry collections, *Soap Is Political* (Glass Lyre, 2015) and *Yellow Doors* (WordFarm, 2003), and her poems have appeared in *RHINO, Calyx, Iron Horse Literary Review, Crab Orchard Review*, and elsewhere. Her 2017 children's picture book is *Adriana's Angels / Los ángeles de Adriana* (Sparkhouse Family). She edits books at the University of Chicago Press and is currently creating art for a book tentatively titled *Picturing God*, due out fall 2019.

Pamela Gibbs Hirschler is a native Kentuckian who writes poetry and fiction. Her work has appeared in *Pine Mountain Sand & Gravel, Talking River, The Heartland Review, Still: The Journal,* and the anthologies *See How We Are* and *Her Limestone Bones*. She holds an MFA in Poetry from Drew University.

Susan Hodgin, a semi-retired language arts teacher and Southeastern Louisiana native, moved to Idaho with her husband D'Wayne in 1977. Living on the Palouse Prairie, they enjoy the amenities of Moscow and the University of Idaho, where they found the richness of community, the haven for their Idaho family and Newfoundlands. This past summer marks Susan's three-year appointment by the Moscow Arts Commission as Moscow, Idaho's second poet laureate.

Akua Lezli Hope is a creator who uses sound, words, fiber, glass, metal and pigment to create poems, patterns, stories, music, sculpture, adornments and peace whenever possible. She has published 121 crochet designs and founded a paratransit nonprofit. Her awards include fellowships from the New York Foundation for the Arts, Ragdale, and The National Endowment for the Arts. Her new poetry collection is *THEM GONE* (The Word Works, 2018).

Kate Hovey has authored three award-winning books of poetry for young readers: *Arachne Speaks, Ancient Voices* and *Voices of the Trojan War* (Simon and Schuster). A contributor to *Women Versed in Myth: Essays on Modern Poets* (McFarland), her work is forthcoming or has appeared most recently in *Nasty Women Poets: An Unapologetic Anthology of Subversive Verse* (Lost Horse Press), *Fiolet and Wing: An Anthology of Domestic Fabulist Poetry* and *Beyond the Lyric Moment* (Tebot Bach).

JP Howard's debut poetry collection, *SAY/MIRROR* (The Operating System), was a Lambda Literary finalist. She is the author of *bury your love poems here* (Belladonna*). JP is a 2018 featured author in Lambda Literary's LGBTQ Writers in Schools program and was a Split This Rock Freedom Plow Award for Poetry & Activism finalist. JP has received fellowships from Cave Canem, VONA, and Lambda and curates Women Writers in Bloom Poetry Salon. jp-howard.com

Siham Karami's first full-length collection is *To Love the River* (Kelsay Books 2018), and her chapbook manuscript *Whore of Blue* was a finalist in the QuillsEdge chapbook competition. Her work has appeared in *The Comstock Review, Able Muse, Off the Coast, The Rumpus, Pleiades,* and *Anti-Heroin Chic*, among others. Nominated multiple times for the Pushcart Prize and Best of the Net, she blogs at sihamkarami.wordpress.com.

Helena Kim lives and writes on the island of Hawaii. She is a poet and fiction writer. Her poetry has been published in the *Global City Review* and *Noyo River Review*. Her novel, *The Long Season of Rain*, (under Helen Kim) was nominated for a National Book Award and was translated into seven languages for both adult and young adult. She is the recipient of a New Jersey State Council on the Arts grant.

A graduate of Drew University, MFA in Poetry, **Gail Langstroth** is an international lecturer, eurythmy performer, poet and film artist. She lives in Pittsburgh, PA, where she is an active member of the Madwomen in the Attic writing workshops. THE HEART BETWEEN HAMMERS, based on Rilke's *Duino Elegies*, and *firegarden / jardín-de-fuego*, a performance piece inspired by poems in her duo-language manuscript of the same title, account for some of her most recent stage productions. wordmoves.com

Professor **Mary Catherine Loving** completed a PhD in the Humanities. She publishes poetry, critical essays and opinion pieces. Her most recent essay is on Lucille Clifton's use of names and is published by Palgrave MacMillan.

Janet MacFadyen is author of *Waiting to Be Born* (Dos Madres Press) and *A Newfoundland Journal* (Killick Press), along with two chapbooks. Her work appears widely and has received nominations for the Forward and Pushcart Prizes. In addition to a fellowship at the Provincetown Fine Arts Work Center, she has had residencies at Cill Rialaig (Ireland) and several dune shacks. She is the managing editor of the poetry collaborative, Slate Roof Press.

Katharyn Howd Machan, author of 37 collections of poetry, has lived in Ithaca, New York, since 1975 and, now as a full professor, has taught Writing at Ithaca College since 1977. After many years of coordinating the Ithaca Community Poets and directing the Feminist Women's Writing Workshops, Inc., she was selected to be Tompkins County's first poet laureate. Her poems have appeared in numerous magazines, anthologies, and textbooks, and she has edited three thematic anthologies.

Born from sun, water, and waves in Havana, Cuba, **Mariel Masque**'s poetry frames her queer Mestiza surreal world and uses her Caribbean, Spanish, and Moorish roots to weave rhymes that reclaim and celebrate her mixed heritage and bridge her diverse cultures, roots, and beliefs. Anthologized in Canada and the US, Mariel is a member of the Latina writers group, Mujeres Que Escriben and lives in Oro Valley, Arizona with her gatos Magia, Oráculo y Aragon.

Lynne McEniry, author of *some other wet landscape* published by Get Fresh Books, LLC, was nominated for a Pushcart Prize and twice recognized for the Allen Ginsberg Award. Her poems are in journals, anthologies, and collaborative projects with painters, dancers, and animators. Lynne co-hosts a reading series for Arts By The People and edits for journals and presses. Born in Yonkers, NY, Lynne lives in Morristown, NJ, and works at The College of Saint Elizabeth.

JC Miller's poetry has appeared in the *Iron Horse Literary Review, Summerset Review, cahoodaloodaling, Mojave River Review* and *Pittsburgh Poetry Review* among others. A nominee for Best New Poets and Best of the Net, she received a 2014 grant from the Delaware DOA. Miller was a finalist in the 2017 Red Wheelbarrow Poetry Contest and the 2018 Florence C. Coltman Award.

Ruth Mota lives and writes in the Santa Cruz Mountains of California, and leads poetry circles for veterans and for men incarcerated in a nearby jail. Although she studied English at Oberlin College, her advanced degree is in Public Health and most of her published writing relates to her work as an international HIV/AIDS trainer. Her published poems are about nature or reflect her experiences living and working in Brazil and Africa. She is pictured here with her friend Pechisso, of "Pechisso's Tale."

Bo Niles is a former magazine editor/writer who concentrated on home design. She began writing poetry at 92nd Street Y workshops in New York City, and is now a member of the 92Y's senior poetry group. Her poems have appeared in a number of journals and anthologies, plus three chapbooks—*intimate geographies, natural causes,* and *crescendo | decrescendo*—from Finishing Line Press in Kentucky. She has two grown sons, one married, and two grandchildren.

Over the years **Faith Paulsen** has held day jobs as a technical writer, travel writer, freelance writer and in the insurance industry to support her family and her selfish and expensive writing habit. Her work has appeared in a variety of venues ranging in alphabetical order from *Apiary* to *Wild River Review*. One poem was nominated for a Pushcart. Her first chapbook, *A Color Called Harvest* (Finishing Line Press), was published in 2016.

Nadine Pinede writes poetry of place and displacement. Her parents fled dictatorship in Haiti, where her family tree includes artists, publishers, and an American Revolutionary War hero. Nadine is the first Haitian-American Rhodes Scholar and author of an *An Invisible Geography, Sexism & Race* and *Women in Film*. A Pushcart Prize nominee, her work appears in *Haiti Noir, Spoon River Poetry Review*, and *On Being*. Nadine and her husband live near Belgium's primeval beech forest.

Phyllis Price's poetry reflects the deep connection between humanity and the natural world. Her work has appeared in anthologies and the literary journals *Poem, Connecticut River Review, Appalachian Heritage,* and *Greensboro Review,* among others. Price is the author of chapbook *Quarry Song* (Finishing Line Press, 2016) and spiritual autobiography *Holy Fire* (Paulist Press, 1996). She resides in her native southwest Virginia among family, friends, two sheep and a few good hens.

Julie Rochlin is a recent finalist for a New Millennium Poetry prize. She's been published in *Chautauqua* among other journals and was nominated for a Pushcart Prize. She lives in Cambridge, Massachusetts where she's part of an eco-friendly co-housing community. At a time when women's voices are rising to the forefront, she's honored to be included in this inaugural anthology.

Joanna Rose has published stories, essays, poems, and a novel called *Little Miss Strange* (Algonquin), as well as other pieces that don't fall into any of those categories. Her work has appeared in many small journals. She teaches youth through Literary Arts Writers in the Schools and Young Musicians & Artists. When she's not at the beach, she lives in downtown Portland.

Katherine DiBella Seluja is a poet and a nurse practitioner. Her work has appeared in the *American Journal of Nursing, basque, Intima* and *Iron Horse Literary Review,* among others. Her first collection, *Gather the Night*, focuses on the impact of mental illness and is forthcoming from UNM Press. Her collaborative manuscript, *We Are Meant to Carry Water*, written with Tina Carlson and Stella Reed, is forthcoming from 3: A Taos Press. Katherine lives in New Mexico.

Margie Shaheed is a community poet, writer and teaching artist. Her work has been published recently in *Mad River Review, Mom Egg Review* and *Bookends Review*. She has four poetry chapbooks in print. Her first nonfiction book, *Tongue Shakers: Interviews and Narratives on Speaking Mother Tongue in a Multicultural Society* was published by Hamilton Books, 2017. She is the proud grandmother of four grandsons.

Amy Small-McKinney won The Kithara Book Prize 2016 (Glass Lyre Press) for her second full-length poetry collection, *Walking Toward Cranes*. Her poems have appeared in numerous journals, for example, *American Poetry Review* and *The Cortland Review*. Her poems were translated into Korean in the bilingual anthology, *Bridging the Waters II*, published by Cross-Cultural Communications. She facilitates community poetry workshops in Philadelphia and taught at the 2018 Philadelphia Writers' Conference.

Rose M. Smith is author of four chapbooks, most recently *Holes in My Teeth* (Kattywampus Press, 2016). Her work appears in *Minola Review, Mom Egg Review, pluck!, Naugatuck River Review, Snapdragon, Main Street Rag,* and *The Pedestal Magazine,* among others. She's served with Ohio Arts Council's Poetry Out Loud program for several years. Rose is a Senior Editor with Pudding Magazine and a graduate Cave Canem fellow. Her collection *Unearthing Ida* won the 2018 Lyrebird Prize from Glass Lyre Press.

Judith Sornberger's newest poetry book, *Practicing the World*, is from CavanKerry Press (2018). She's the author of one other full-length poetry collection, *Open Heart* (Calyx Books), and five chapbooks, most recently *Wal-Mart Orchid*, winner of the 2012 Helen Kay Chapbook Prize (Evening Street Press). Her prose memoir, *The Accidental Pilgrim: Finding God and His Mother in Tuscany,* was published by Shanti Arts Press in 2015.

Lynne Santy Tanner graduated from Hollins College in Roanoke, Virginia, with a Bachelor of Arts in Biology and a minor in Dance. She has been choreographer for the Rutherford County, North Carolina, Arts Council for more than forty-five years. Finishing Line Press published her chapbooks: *Where There Is No Night* (2004), *Carilee's House* (2006) and *The Brown Thrasher* (2013). She lives in North Carolina with her husband.

Eileen Toomey fell in love with writing through the Writing Workshop at Columbia College, Chicago. She has her BA from the University of Baltimore. She has had one poem published in *the museum of americana*, and personal essays in *The Eastern Iowa Review, Fish Food Magazine,* and *The Rumpus.*

Gina Valdés was born in Los Angeles and grew up on both sides of the United States-Mexico border. Since 1975, she has been steadily publishing poetry in journals and anthologies in the U.S., Mexico, and Europe. Most recently, her work appeared in *Calyx, Earth's Daughters, Spillways, Huizache,* and *Mizna*. She's the author of two bilingual chapbooks, *Comiendo lumbre / Eating Fire* and *Puentes y fronteras / Bridges and Borders* (Bilingual Press).

Lynn Valente taught Spanish in a small rural high school. Following retirement, she has been writing, playing music, and enjoying the natural world. She lives in Vermont.

Wendy Marie Vergoz teaches English at Marian University, and leads a community writing workshop for women survivors of incarceration, domestic violence, and addiction. Vergoz has received a Creative Renewal Arts Fellowship from the Arts Council of Indianapolis and an Individual Artist Grant from the Indiana Arts Commission. Her poems have appeared in *Cleaver Magazine, Flying Island, Ground, The Christian Century, Literary Mama,* and *Anglican Theological Review* and in multiple artistic exhibitions.

Tori Grant Welhouse is a Wisconsin poet, writer, photographer, active volunteer with Wisconsin Fellowship of Poets (wfop.org) and co-collaborator on *Bramble Literary Magazine*. She earned an MFA from Antioch International in London and published a poetry chapbook, *Canned*, with Finishing Line Press. Her poetry has also appeared in *Anderbo, Midwest Prairie Review, Passager, ROAR, Rivet* and others. torigrantwelhouse.com

NOTES

BRENDA BELL BROWN, KEEP A MESSY HOUSE:
"dust from the foot of a generous woman, Lord Krishna, dust from her foot will cure you"—line spoken by actor Josh Hartnett as Jude in the film "The Ottoman Lieutenant"

AMY SMALL-MCKINNEY, POEM BEGINNING WITH A LINE BY DAISY ZAMORA:
"I am looking for the women of my house."—Daisy Zamora, from "Lineage"

GAIL LANGSTROTH, *NEGATIVE INCURSIONS:* RULA HALAWANI'S PHOTOGRAPH:
Poem inspired by Rula Halawani's photograph in her series "Negative Incursions from Rawiya," featured in the exhibition *She Who Tells a Story: Women Photographers from Iran and the Arab World*, The Carnegie Mellon Museum of Art, Pittsburgh, PA, September 2015

ROSE M. SMITH, BLOOD FROM THE SON:
In May, 2017, long after the birth of this poem, the city of Milwaukee proposed a $2.3 million settlement to be held in trust for Dontre's young son.

RUTH GORING, CANCIONCITAS DE REMIENDAS/SMALL SONGS FOR MENDING:
Ruth originally wrote this poem in Spanish, and later translated it into English.

KATE HOVEY, LILITH UTTERS INEFFABLE NAMES:
Italicized phrases are text from the Bible (RSV), *The Magus,* or *Celestial Intelligencer* (Francis Barrett, 1801) and *The Alphabet of Ben Sira.*

JOANNE GODLEY, BOIS CAIMAN CEREMONY:
Bois Caïman (lit. Cayman Woods; Kreyòl: Bwa Kayiman) is the site of the vodou ceremony presided over by Boukman Dutty and Cecile Fatiman on August 14, 1791. It is widely accepted as the starting point for the Haitian Revolution.